PENGUIN BOOKS

JOURNAL OF A NOVEL

T0228656

Born in Salinas, California, in 190
in a fertile agricultural valley abc
the Pacific Coast—and both valley and coast would serve as
settings for some of his best fiction. In 1919 he went to
Stanford University, where he intermittently enrolled in
literature and writing courses until he left in 1925 without
taking a degree. During the next five years he supported
himself as a laborer and journalist in New York City and then
as a caretaker for a Lake Tahoe estate, all the time working
on his first novel, *Cup of Gold* (1929). After marriage and a
move to Pacific Grove, he published two California fic-
tions, *The Pastures of Heaven* (1932) and *To a God Unknown*
(1933), and worked on short stories later collected in *The
Long Valley* (1938). Popular success and financial security
came only with *Tortilla Flat* (1935), stories about Monterey's
paisanos. A ceaseless experimenter throughout his career,
Steinbeck changed courses regularly. Three powerful novels
of the late 1930s focused on the California laboring class:
In Dubious Battle (1936), *Of Mice and Men* (1937), and the
book considered by many his finest, *The Grapes of Wrath*
(1939). Early in the 1940s, Steinbeck became a filmmaker
with *The Forgotten Village* (1941) and a serious student of
marine biology with *Sea of Cortez*. He devoted his services to
the war, writing *Bombs Away* (1942) and the controversial
play-novelette *The Moon Is Down* (1942). *Cannery Row*
(1945), *The Wayward Bus* (1947), *The Pearl* (1947), *A Rus-
sian Journal* (1948), another experimental drama, *Burning
Bright* (1950), and *The Log from the* Sea of Cortez (1951)
preceded publication of the monumental *East of Eden*
(1952), an ambitious saga of the Salinas Valley and his own
family's history. The last decades of his life were spent in
New York City and Sag Harbor with his third wife, with
whom he traveled widely. Later books include *Sweet Thursday* (1954), *The Short Reign of Pippin IV: A Fabrication*
(1957), *Once There Was a War* (1958), *The Winter of Our
Discontent* (1961), *Travels with Charley in Search of America*
(1962), *America and Americans* (1966), and the posthu-
mously published *Journal of a Novel: The* East of Eden *Letters*
(1969), *Viva Zapata!* (1975), *The Acts of King Arthur and His
Noble Knights* (1976), and *Working Days: The Journals of*
The Grapes of Wrath (1989). He died in 1968, having won a
Nobel Prize in 1962.

JOURNAL OF A NOVEL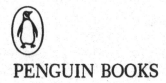

The *East of Eden* Letters

JOHN STEINBECK

PENGUIN BOOKS

PENGUIN BOOKS
Published by the Penguin Group
Penguin Putnam Inc., 375 Hudson Street,
New York, New York 10014, U.S.A.
Penguin Books Ltd, 80 Strand, London WC2R 0RL, England
Penguin Books Australia Ltd, 250 Camberwell Road,
Camberwell, Victoria 3124, Australia
Penguin Books Canada Ltd, 10 Alcorn Avenue,
Toronto, Ontario, Canada M4V 3B2
Penguin Books India (P) Ltd, 11 Community Centre,
Panchsheel Park, New Delhi – 110 017, India
Penguin Books (N.Z.) Ltd, Cnr Rosedale and Airborne Roads,
Albany, Auckland, New Zealand
Penguin Books (South Africa) (Pty) Ltd, 24 Sturdee Avenue,
Rosebank, Johannesburg 2196, South Africa

Penguin Books Ltd, Registered Offices:
Harmondsworth, Middlesex, England

First published in the United States of America by
The Viking Press, Inc., 1969
Published in a Viking Compass Edition 1972
Published in Pengun Books 1990

10

LIBRARY OF CONGRESS CATALOGING IN PUBLICATION DATA
Steinbeck, John, 1902–1968.
Journal of a novel: the East of Eden letters/John Steinbeck.
p.   cm.
ISBN 0 14 01.4418 8
1. Steinbeck, John, 1902–1968. East of Eden.   2. Steinbeck, John,
1902–1968 – Diaries.   3. Novelists, American – 20th century – Diaries.
I. Title.
PS3537.T3234E335   1990
813'.52 – dc20   90–39044

Printed in the United States of America

Contents

Publishers' Note   vii

The Text of the Journal   3

To Pascal Covici   179

Publishers' Note

Emerson has said that when his writing was blocked, he would sit down and write a long letter to a friend whom he loved. John Steinbeck, in writing *East of Eden*, unblocked himself for the daily stint ahead by writing a "letter" to his close friend and editor, Pascal Covici. It was written on the blue-ruled pages of a large notebook, size 10¾" x 14", which Covici had supplied. After the two opening letters, which filled the first few pages continuously, the letters appeared only on the left-hand pages; on the right, when Steinbeck felt ready, he proceeded to the text of the novel. He usually filled two pages of the text a day with a total of about fifteen hundred words. Both the letter and the text were written in black pencil in Steinbeck's minute but clear longhand. The writing covered the period from January 29 through November 1, 1951. There was a letter for every working day until the first draft of the novel was finished.

The letter was primarily a method of warming up, flexing the author's muscles both physical and mental. He sometimes used it to adumbrate the problems and purposes of the passage on which he was about to embark: "a kind of arguing ground for the story," as he says once. If the argument had been worked out in his mind in advance, the material of the letter might consist of random thoughts, trial flights of wordsmanship, nuggets of information and comment for his friend about the surrounding events of the moment, both personal and public. But the letters were also full of serious thinking about this novel, his longest and most ambitious; about novel-writing in general; and about some of Steinbeck's deepest convictions. Not a formal act of literary creation for its own sake, this document casts a flood of light on the author's mind and on the nature of the creative process. And in its private glimpses of the Nobel Prize-winning writer—his concern about his sons, his hobbies such as wood-carving and carpentry, his passion for invention—it is autobiographical material of the first order. In a sense this is Steinbeck's Testament.

Taken simply as a document, which he did not intend for publication and never revised in any way, it is probably unique. Its repetitions, even its seeming irrelevancies, are a part of its documentary interest. The text printed here follows the carefully typed transcription made from the original longhand by Mrs. Dorothy Covici for her husband, and no attempt has been made now to check it back word for word against the original longhand (a task for later scholars) except at a few points where she had been uncertain of the handwriting. It is published here intact as a reading version, without editing except in two minor respects. A few lines here and there, as indicated [. . .], have been omitted in deference to the feelings of living people, and a few inconsistencies in spelling, obvious slips of the pencil, and hasty punctuation have been corrected. Steinbeck was normally permissive with his editors on such points, though he strongly resisted what he called "collaboration" on more important matters. *

The letters, of course, refer to the first draft of *East of Eden*. After it was copied by a typist, Steinbeck made extensive revisions, omitted whole passages, and rearranged some of the chapters. The task of correlating the letters with the published text of the novel must also await future scholarship. Here, footnotes are supplied only in a few cases where references to the original text might be puzzling.

The publishers are deeply indebted to Mrs. Elaine Steinbeck for her cooperation in elucidating references not clear in context and supplying identifications added in footnotes. They are also grateful to the Humanities Research Center of the University of Texas at Austin, the present owners, for permitting photographs of the original manuscript to be made for the sample facsimile pages; and to Pascal Covici, Jr., for permission to photograph the box

---

* Although Steinbeck's spelling in general was exceptionally good, he consistently spelled the word "rhythm" without the first "h"; usually inserted an apostrophe in the possessive pronoun "its" while omitting it from the contraction "it's"; omitted the apostrophe from "the day's work" and the like; tended to make two words of such compounds as "background" and wrote "of course" as if it were one. Only changes of this very minor order have been made here. The datelines have been made uniform in style, except that when Steinbeck wrote the wrong day or date, or omitted it, the correct one has been supplied in brackets.

which Steinbeck carved to hold the manuscript and then gave to his editor. Finally they wish to express their gratitude to Steinbeck's two sons, Thom Steinbeck ("Tom" in the script) and John Steinbeck IV ("Catbird"). In the first of the letters to Covici, and also in letters addressed to them and intended to go in the book but later omitted, their father made clear to what a great extent he was motivated by the boys, six and four years old when the letters begin, in writing *East of Eden.*

Also printed here for the first time is the "dedication, prologue, argument, apology, epilogue and perhaps epitaph all in one" which Steinbeck originally drafted for the book as a prefatory letter to Pascal Covici. In the end he decided to substitute the simpler and more personal dedication that appears in the published novel. The imaginary conversation in this draft was just that—an argument which Steinbeck facetiously set up in anticipation of what he feared might be said about the book by his publishers and the reader. Needless to say, it never took place. But it tells much about author-publisher relationships.

JOURNAL OF A NOVEL

January 29, 1951 [MONDAY]

Dear Pat: How did the time pass and how did it grow so late. Have we learned anything from the passage of time? Are we more mature, wiser, more perceptive, kinder? We have known each other now for centuries and still I remember the first time and the last time.

We come now to the book. It has been planned a long time. I planned it when I didn't know what it was about. I developed a language for it that I will never use. This seems such a waste of the few years a man has to write in. And still I do not think I could have written it before now. Of course it would have been a book—but not this book. I remember when you gave me this thick—black—expensive book to write in. See how well I have kept it for this book. Only six pages are out of it. A puppy gnawed the corners of the front cover. And it is clean and fresh and open. I hope I can fill it as you would like it filled.

The last few years have been painful. I don't know whether they have hurt permanently or not. Certainly they have changed me. I would have been stone if they had not. I hope they have not taken too much away from me. Now I am married to Elaine and in two days I am moving into the pretty little house on 72nd St. and there I will have a room to work in and I will have love all around me. Maybe I can finally write this book. All the experiment is over now. I either write the book or I do not. There can be no excuses. The form will not be startling, the writing will be spare and lean, the concepts hard, the philosophy old and yet new born. In a sense it will be two books—the story of my county and the story of me. And I shall keep these two separate. It may be that they should not be printed together. But that we will have to see after the book is all over and finished and with it a great part of me.

I am choosing to write this book to my sons. They are little boys now and they will never know what they came from through me, unless I tell them. It is not written for them to read now but when they are grown and the pains and joys have tousled them a little. And if the book is addressed to them, it is for a good reason. I want them to know how it was, I want to tell them directly, and perhaps by speaking directly to them I shall speak directly to other people. One can go off into fanciness if one writes to a huge nebulous group but I think it will be necessary to speak very straight and clearly and simply if I address my book to two little boys who will be men before they read my book. They have no background in the world of literature, they don't know the great stories of the world as we do. And so I will tell them one of the greatest, perhaps the greatest story of all—the story of good and evil, of strength and weakness, of love and hate, of beauty and ugliness. I shall try to demonstrate to them how these doubles are inseparable—how neither can exist without the other and how out of their groupings creativeness is born. I shall tell them this story against the background of the county I grew up in and along the river I know and do not love very much. For I have discovered that there are other rivers. And this my boys will not know for a long time nor can they be told. A great many never come to know that there are other rivers. Perhaps that knowledge is saved for maturity and very few people ever mature. It is enough if they flower and reseed. That is all that nature requires of them. But sometimes in a man or a woman awareness takes place—not very often and always inexplainable. There are no words for it because there is no one ever to tell. This is a secret not kept a secret, but locked in wordlessness. The craft or art of writing is the clumsy attempt to find symbols for the wordlessness. In utter loneliness a writer tries to explain the inexplicable. And sometimes if he is very fortunate and if the time is right, a very little of what he is trying to do trickles through—not ever much. And if he is a writer wise enough to know it can't be done, then he is not a writer at all. A good writer always works at the impossible. There is another kind who pulls in his horizons, drops his mind as one lowers rifle sights. And giving up the impossible he gives up writing. Whether fortunate or unfortunate, this has not happened to me. The same blind effort, the straining and puffing go on in me. And always I hope that a little trickles through. This urge dies hard.

This book will be the most difficult of all I have ever attempted. Whether I am good enough or gifted enough remains to be seen. I do have a good background. I have love and I have had pain. I still have anger but I can find no bitterness in myself. There may be some bitterness but if there is I don't know where it can be. I do not seem to have the kind of selfness any more that nourishes it.

And so I will start my book addressed to my boys. I think perhaps it is the only book I have ever written. I think there is only one book to a man. It is true that a man may change or be so warped that he becomes another man and has another book but I do not think that is so with me.

February 12 [MONDAY]

As I said above, we moved into the little house on 72nd St. We have been painting and carrying and arranging for over a week. But there has to come a day when one says—"Now that is over." I can do many small things after 3:30 but the first part of the day must now be for the book. This is a kind of necessary selfishness—otherwise books do not get written. And so I am taking this Lincoln's Birthday of 1951 to start my book. I will be 49 in two weeks. I am fairly strong but breathless. I weigh somewhat too much and will try to lose a little weight as I go. Because of all the confusion of the last several years, I will have difficulty in concentrating for a while. That is a conditioned trick. My health is generally good. I have been drinking too much, I think, and a few times in the last months I have had depressions. But it does not seem to me that the depressions are as awful as they used to be. Perhaps some acid juice is drying up. My sexual drive is, if anything, stronger than ever but that may be because it is all in one direction now and not scattered. I don't know about my thinking. It will take this book to determine whether or not that is any good. My mind seems to me to be young and elastic but perhaps everyone thinks that always.

I am trying to set down the condition I start with. I intend to keep a double-entry book—manuscript on the right-hand page and work diary on the left. Thus they will be together. I guess that brings me to the end of this opening letter. We will have to see whether the practicing through the years has prepared me for the writing of a book. For this is the book I have always wanted and have worked and prayed to be able to write. We shall see whether I am capable. Surely I feel humble in the face of this work.

And as our Roman friends would say when casting outside themselves for help, *Ora pro mihi*.

February 12, *continued*

Lincoln's Birthday. My first day of work in my new room. It is a very pleasant room and I have a drafting table to work on which I have always wanted—also a comfortable chair given me by Elaine. In fact I have never had it so good and so comfortable. It does occur to me that perhaps it might be a little too comfortable. I have known such things to happen—the perfect pointed pencil—the paper persuasive—the fantastic chair and a good light and no writing. Surely a man is a most treacherous animal full of his treasured contradictions. He may not admit it but he loves his paradoxes.

Now that I have everything, we shall see whether I have anything. It is exactly that simple. Mark Twain used to write in bed—so did our greatest poet. But I wonder how often they wrote in bed—or whether they did it twice and the story took hold. Such things happen. Also I would like to know what things they wrote in bed and what things they wrote sitting up. All of this has to do with comfort in writing and what its value is. I should think that a comfortable body would let the mind go freely to its gathering. But such is the human that he might react in an opposite. Remember my father's story about the man who did not dare be comfortable because he went to sleep. That might be true of me too. Now I am perfectly comfortable in body. I think my house is in order. Elaine, my beloved, is taking care of all the outside details to allow me the amount of free untroubled time every day to do my work. I can't think of anything else necessary to a writer except a story and the will and the ability to tell it.

In considering this book and in planning for it I have thought of many great and interesting tricks. I have made new languages, new symbols, a new kind of writing; and now that the book is ready to go, I am throwing them all away and starting from scratch. I want to make this book so simple in its difficulty that a child can understand it. I want to go through it before it is typed and take out even the few adjectives I have let slip in. What then will the style be? I don't know. Books establish their own pace. This I have found out. As soon as the story starts its style will establish itself. But still I do not think that all the experimenting is wasted that has kept some aliveness. The waggling pencil—the apes with typewriters hitting at a dictionary—this has been all right but it cannot be depended on.

Now I come down to exactness. Before too long I am going to have to write Chapter I. And it must have its design made in advance. What is it that I want to say in my opening? First I want to establish the boys—what they are and what they are like. Then I would like to indicate my reason for writing this book to them. Then I would like in general terms to tell them what their blood is. Next I want to describe the Salinas Valley in detail but in sparse detail so that there can be a real feeling of it. It should be sights and sounds, smells and colors but put down with simplicity as though the boys were able to read it. This is the physical background of the book. Next our grandfather* and his sons and his daughters and his wife and the land they took up near King City and how they lived, and some attempt to give them a quality of their background. And finally I want to mention the neighbors. I do not have the name yet. I think it might be Canable. No, that is a double or rather a triple meaning I don't want. The name is so important that I want to think about it. I remember a friend of my father's—a whaling master named Captain Trask. I have always loved the name. It meant great romance to me. Anyway, the last part of the first chapter will refer to the Trasks and their place. Then the second chapter will begin the Trask story. In the opening there must be the techniques of living to a certain extent. Then as the book progresses, it is my intention, every other chapter, to continue the letter to the boys with all of the thinking and the detail necessary for one to understand the main story of three generations of Trasks. The advantage of this will be that the story itself can be increasingly quick and terse and short. Such readers as only like plot and dialogue can then skip every other chapter and meanwhile I can take time for thought, comment, observation, criticism, and if it should seem a good thing to throw it out, I can do that too. Or it could be put in a second book. Actually it will be a kind of parallel biography. And it may well be that a great deal of it may be thrown out. But that we will see as we go along. I don't want to

---

* The first page of the novel faced the first page of this letter, which ended here in the manuscript. It was headed: THE SALINAS VALLEY, and began: "Dear Tom and John." The opening paragraphs, and other letters addressed to the boys, persisted through the first draft but were later omitted. The plan to make the chapters alternate rigidly between the Trasks and the Hamiltons, and to address all the Hamilton chapters to the boys, was abandoned earlier.

dawdle too much today and on the other hand I do not want to start the book today. I want to get all the thinking detail of the first chapter done. And that is it. The physical valley—then center down to the little area. But try to relate the reader to the book so that, while I am talking to the boys actually, I am relating every reader to the story as though he were reading about his own background. If I can do that, it will be very helpful. Everyone wants to have a family. Maybe I can create a universal family living next to a universal neighbor. This should not be impossible.

I am using up such quantities of my free space that I will not have space for the writing. But on my first day, which will be tomorrow, I will have to fill three pages. For tomorrow there will be nothing in this left-hand page except field notes.

I have a good feeling about this book now and I hope I can keep it. It is a feeling of real relaxation and rest. It would be fine if I could keep such a feeling. I surely intend to try. Next, I want to be so relaxed that the book will soothe and excite at the same time. Also it must not be a dour book but one that has gaiety as well as movement. It has to have a universal quality or there is no point in writing it.

The writing table is perfect. I have never been so content with anything. And the blue wing-back chair is wonderfully comfortable. It might possibly be too comfortable but this I do not believe. I think that if I can be relaxed, the book has a chance of being relaxed, and I have a very strong feeling about this book being completely at ease and comfortable. Also I have a strong feeling about its being very long. Otherwise I will have lost my whole direction. I want to take a great time with this book. I would like to write on it all year—if that seems good. I know that you, Pat, are anxious to get it done and out but that is because then the work you love will start. But this book is to be the labor that I love and I intend to take full advantage of it. I have often thought that this might be my last book. I don't really mean that because I will be writing books until I die. But I want to write this one *as though* it were my last book. Maybe I believe that every book should be written that way. I think I mean that. It is the ideal. And I have done just the opposite. I have written each book as an exercise, as practice for the one to come. And this is the one to come. There is nothing beyond this book—nothing follows it. It must contain all in the world I know and it must have everything in it of which I am capable—all styles, all techniques, all poetry—and it must have in it a great deal of laughter. I can see no reason why I should not tell the family stories. They are just as good as they ever were and maybe as I go I will remember more and more of them. But I do know that I must put in all of the lore and anecdote I can. And many of my family stories amount to folklore and should be used for and by the boys. Then they will know their family. I think I will put a good deal of my mother and my father also. It is time I wrote these things, else they will be gone because no one else will ever do them except me. I am very happy at my new table and with all my things about me. Never have I had such a comfortable layout.

My choice of pencils lies now between the black Calculator stolen from Fox Films and this Mongol 2⅜ F which is quite black and holds its point well—much better in fact than the Fox pencils. I will get six more or maybe four more dozens of them for my pencil tray. And this is all I am going to do on this my first day of work.

February 13 [TUESDAY]

It must be told that my second work day is a bust as far as getting into the writing. I suffer as always from the fear of putting down the first line. It is amazing the terrors, the magics, the prayers, the straightening shyness that assails one. It is as though the words were not only indelible but that they spread out like dye in water and color everything around them. A strange and mystic business, writing. Almost no progress has taken place since it was invented. The Book of the Dead is as good and as highly developed as anything in the 20th century and much better than most. And yet in spite of this lack of a continuing excellence, hundreds of thousands of people are in my shoes—praying feverishly for relief from their word pangs.

And one thing we have lost—the courage to make new words or combinations. Somewhere that old bravado has slipped off into a gangrened scholarship. Oh! you can make words if you enclose them in quotation marks. This indicates that it is dialect and cute.

I have a weary little weight on my head today. Last night I could not sleep out of excitement about my story. It was a strange voluptuous excitement and when I dropped off I had a quick sex dream, perhaps because my feeling was exotic. Now I am slipping so far ahead of the pages for narrative but there's no harm in that. I have said to myself that this book must be unhurried and serene. And if these observations can promote the calm I want, then I am

9

willing to go along with it indefinitely. I am pleased with myself for no reason at all. I have a good golden light in my stomach which is a mesh of happiness. Isn't that odd and delightful? Every once in a while I get the feeling that this is a secret book like some of the others that were kept in a gloom and burned straight, and a good thing too for they carried uncreative misery and there is no good in that at all. How different now—maybe I'm fooling myself. That is always possible but I do indeed seem to feel creative juices rushing toward an outlet as semen gathers from the four quarters of a man and fights its way into the vesicle. I hope something beautiful and true comes out—but this I know (and the likeness to coition still holds). Even if I knew nothing would emerge from this book I would still write it. It seems to me that different organisms must have their separate ways of symbolizing, with sound or gesture, the creative joy—the flowering. And if this is so, men also must have their separate ways—some to laugh and some to build, some to destroy and yes, some even creatively to destroy themselves. There's no explaining this. The joy thing in me has two outlets: one a fine charge of love toward the incredibly desirable body and sweetness of woman, and second—mostly both—the paper and pencil or pen. And it is interesting to think what paper and pencil and the wriggling words are. They are nothing but the trigger into joy—the shout of beauty—the cacajada of the pure bliss of creation. And often the words do not even parallel the feeling except sometimes in intensity. Thus a man full of a bursting joy may write with force and vehemence of some sad picture —of the death of beauty or the destruction of a lovely town—and there is only the effectiveness to prove how great and beautiful was his feeling.

You might as well get used to this, Pat. I write many thousands of words a day and some of them go on paper. And of those which are written down, only a few are ever meant to be seen. And it occurred to me that since you bought this fine book for me, I would put most of the writing in it. There is still the secret writing which will be burned but that deals with matters I have no wish for anyone to see, even you. But all that can be seen I will put in this book and it may be that half way through my novel, you may be required to buy me another book. How you would hate that.

I see now what I am doing and I do not think it is a waste of time. The body of the book is addressed to my children and for them at any age there must be a reduction to complete simplicity —not because they are stupid but because their experience will have been different from mine. Therefore we must meet on some common ground between. But your experience and mine, while not identical, are near enough so that we can meet on the same ground. And that is probably what I am instinctively doing, coming out of the cold of the strange into the warm of the familiar. Such things seem to be a matter of reflex. In this connection—I can find in notebooks many years old ideas and feelings and even stories I did not know about. For this reason it is not well to attempt to analyse too closely at first—an emotion which falls by some accident into edged words, swings the whole brain about and shakes it like a rug. This happens oftener than we know.

I feel that sometimes when I am writing I am very near to a kind of unconsciousness. Then time does change its manner and minutes disappear into the cloud of time which is one thing, having only one duration. I have thought that if we could put off our duration-preoccupied minds, it might be that time has no duration at all. Then all history and all pre-history might indeed be one durationless flash like an exploding star, eternal and without duration.

So, we move on. My mind blasted just then with an idea so comely, like a girl, so very sweet and dear that I will put her aside for the book. Oh! she is lovely, this idea.

And it is odd also, how one with such benevolence as I can have at the same time, layer on layer, a callous cruelty, capable of almost anything, of death, and hurt—an implacable cruelty needing only a direction as the benevolence does. With a channel, this mind can be a destroying angel. And crazily enough—it's the same mind swinging in the strongest wind, taking its direction from the wind. I don't know whether all minds are like this. Mine is the only one I know about.

Sometimes I am impatient with those who think themselves kind when their only thought is to preserve themselves from the discomfort of observed pain.

February 15 [THURSDAY]

Yesterday was Valentine's Day and I went to the 78th St. house to take the things to the boys.* They were withdrawn and cautious [. . .].

---

* His sons were living with their mother, Gwyndolen Conger, Steinbeck's second wife.

Time now comes finally to move my book. I have dawdled enough. But it has been a good thing. I don't yet know what the word rate will be. That will depend on many things. But I do think the hour rate should be fairly constant. I am about finished with these long and characteristic meanderings. It is with real fear that I go to the other. And I must forget even that I want it to be good. Such things belong only in the planning stage. Once it starts, it should not have any intention save only to be written. All is peace now. And all is quiet. What little things there are, are here and good. Posture and attitude are so very important. And since these things have to go on for a very long time, they must become almost a way of life and a habit of thought. So that no one may say, I lost by being lost. This is the last bounce on the board, the last look into the pool. The time has come for the dive. The time has really come. I'll keep this running comment going but it will be more restricted. Now I must go to the Salinas Valley. And if it can be believed—I am glad to go there on paper rather than in person. Odd how reluctant I am to start. I suppose that everyone hates discipline and fights it off at all costs. How the paper eats up pencil line. How it does.

My son Tom is in trouble in some way. I only know it because I feel it in his eyes and in the quick frantic and quickly covered emotion of yesterday. I don't know what to do but I know I must do something to help him. He has become silent and Gwyn says defiant. I know how that is. Then there is the story that I meet him at school every day to meet him. He wouldn't tell such a story unless he had a definite need of it. And I think I had better go and talk with the people who see him most—the people in school. At least that seems the good thing to me. And now, I must get to work.

February 16, Friday

Just as it always does—the work started without warning. It is always that way. I must sit a certain length of time before it happens. Yesterday it began to come and I think the form is set now. I know it is for the alternate chapters. I only hope I can do as well with the other parts of the alternate. Now I have sat a week. It is Friday and I have sweated out one page and a half. If I did not know this process so well, I would consider it a week of waste. But I know better than that now and I am content. I do not think I have wasted this week. In fact I feel a great gain. There is nothing frantic about the book at all. I have never felt this way before. Somehow, Elaine manages to take the pressures off and to keep them off. Last night I read her the opening and she said she liked it. There was hardly enough to judge but some. And you could get tone from it at least. The pipes are tasting very good. I have a feeling to buy a meerschaum and start coloring it as I do this book. Maybe I will do that. By the time the pipe is brown the book should be done. More magics. I think tomorrow I will look for a meerschaum, a small light one. Saw one in a window the other day but I forget where. Oh! I am so happy—so very happy. I think I have never been so happy in my life. It seems absurd to feel so good about anything. Only the boys trouble me—nothing else. Not the war in Korea—it seems remote. In fact not anything. We are spending a lot of money on the house but I want to—and where else should it be spent? I can't think of a better way to spend it. And I love Elaine unbelievably, incredibly. I think this new life is entirely her doing. What joy.

February 19 [MONDAY]

I did not work nor think over the week end and this was done on purpose. I wanted to get my mind clear of the clutter it has been in. There have been so many things to think about and I wanted particularly to let them run their course. [. . .] I was not happy over the week end for an excellent reason. I drank too much on Saturday night and had a hangover on Sunday, a fine depressed hangover in which nothing seemed any good and I myself seemed the most no good of all. This is a fine example of the depressing quality of alcohol. Today I am over it. If I must do these things I suppose Saturday night is the best time to do them. You, Pat, do not approve of drinking and I don't know that I do either. But I find myself doing it nevertheless.

Time impresses me pretty much now. Time and all the fringes and remnants of time. There's a double aspect to the world—always two and sometimes more faces to external realities. And this increases as we go and the faces become broader and meatier.

Today the house is full of pounding. I remember in the Grapes of Wrath book how I complained about the pounding. And this does not bother me at all. For some reason, it does not seem important to me. It is not aimed at me. I always felt that the other was definitely designed to disturb me. I am sure it was not entirely but to a certain extent there was a pleasure in disturbing me. And now I am sure there is not. I think I will buy a meerschaum pipe and see whether I can age it a delicate lovely brown while I am working on this book. They are very beautiful when they are well handled. And I am going to be here at this desk for a very long time. I can think of no pleasanter way to spend the rest of my life than in this house, with these people and at this drafting board. And now—this is enough of dawdling and I will go to my book.

Now the day's work is done and I don't know whether or not it is good. I can only hope that it is. This book has to be so full of casualness as to be quite disarming. Today I got over the background and appearance and history of the Valley. And tomorrow I must start on the Hamiltons. I can tell all I want about them now because they are all dead and they won't resent the truth about themselves. I think it might be all right too, but it is just a matter of keeping the whole thing in drawing. This is my most complicated and at the same time, my most simple sounding book. And that's all for today.

February 20 [TUESDAY]

Today I am early at work and I want to boost the work to two pages today. It is time for that. I know this is going very slowly but I want it that way. I don't want to rush. I am enjoying this work and I truly want it to be the best I have ever done. There is no reason why it should not have the stature I want. I can hear that in my ears and see it with my eyes and there is no reason why my pencil should not write it. Oh! but watch for terseness. Don't let it ever be adjectivally descriptive. I must hold description to an absolute minimum, must to hold my story and all of its strands together. Just remember that this book is going on forever. I do not intend ever to finish it. And only with this attitude will it progress as I wish it to. I must not let any kind of deadline fall across its pages to change its pace. I know, Pat, that you would like to have it for next winter and that is not possible, or for next spring and that is not quite possible. I have no time to finish this. And I will not make a time.

It is amazing how little I worry. I suppose I should worry

about money and the boys and all such things but I do not. I forget to worry even though I know I should, just to be normal. And right in the middle of the attempt I get to thinking about something else. Now it is time to get down to work. I must introduce Samuel Hamilton and his wife to the Salinas Valley. I am pleased now because the geography and weather are over and I can start with the people. It was my intention, Pat, to give rather an impression of the Valley than a detailed account—more a sense of it than anything else. I do hope I have succeeded but I won't know that for a long time. But this book is *not* about geography but about people and I do not want to give the place undue importance. Time to work now.

Work finished for today and the Hamiltons are in. I do hope they are well in. I've worked long today but happily. And now Elaine and I are going to Macy's to look at some grass rugs.

February 21 [WEDNESDAY]

This morning I am remiss, Pat, and for no reason that I can see. Went to bed early, slept well—overslept in fact—feel fine but I find myself dawdling about going to work. I will do it of course. This afternoon I have to make a tape for the Voice of America concerning art under dictatorship. I don't know much about it, never having performed any art under a dictatorship, but I have read some things and I have been in dictatorship countries. Of course I feel that any imposed [institution?], even conditioned, is bad and not conducive to the development of the two great foundations of art and science: curiosity and criticism. If you stifle these two, how can any art emerge? And of course the proof is that none does. But I have not much time for such things.

Now you are going out to the west coast. And I hope you have fun. You haven't had a trip for a long time. I well remember one of the first times I met you. You had a black Borsolino hat and a brown brief case and you stayed at the Sir Francis Drake. I remember you coming through the lobby and paying your bill. That's a long time ago and you don't look much different now. And I remember other things about that trip which I suppose it would be better to forget. Better for you I mean. There I guess I have dawdled from work all I can for one day and I will go to work.

Well, I finished, Pat, and finished the first chapter. And now I go to the second chapter which is very different as you will see. It concerns the Trasks whereas the first chapter is about the Hamiltons.

February 22 [THURSDAY]

Today is Washington's Birthday, Pat, and I am not going to have much time to visit with you. Has it struck you that this is a crazy kind of thing? Writing you what amounts to a letter which you won't even see in under a year. It's fun in a way too. In a year many things will happen and I writing here today don't know what they are. But you, when you read this—if you read it—will know what is going to happen because it will have happened. I think that is almost magic. You know on my left hand on the pad just below the little finger, I have a dark brown spot. And on my left foot in a corresponding place I have another one almost the same. One time a Chinese, seeing the spot on my hand, became very much excited and when I told him about the one on my foot he was keenly interested. He said that in Chinese palmistry the hand spot was a sign of the greatest possible good luck and the one on my foot doubled it. These spots are nothing but a dark pigmentation. I've had them from birth. Indeed, they are what is known as birthmarks. But the reason I brought it up is this. For the last year and a half, they have been getting darker. And if I am to believe in my spots, this must mean that the luck is getting better. And sure enough I have Elaine and what better luck could there be. But the spots continue to darken and maybe that means that I am going to have a book too. And that would be great good luck too. And you see, in spite of what I said about having no time, I go right on with my letters.

These Trasks now. They fascinate me. I know them so thoroughly and I have gone into their ancestry. I know their moods and their impulses perhaps better than I know my own—surely better than my own. It is probable that my own would be a mystery to me if I inspected them at all. About the natures of the Trasks and about their symbol meanings I leave you to find out for yourself. There is a key and there are many leads. I think you will discover the story rather quickly for all of its innocent sound on these pages. Now the innocent sound and the slight conceal ment are not done as tricks but simply so that a man can take from this book as much as he can bring to it. It would not be well to confuse an illiterate man with the statement of a rather profound philosophy. On the other hand, such a man might take pleasure in the surface story and even understand the other things in his unconscious. On the third hand—and I have three—your literate and understanding man will take joy of finding the secrets hidden in this book almost as though he searched for treasure, but we must never tell anyone they are here. Let them be found by accident. I have made the mistake of telling my readers before and I will never make that mistake again. You will notice my methods of trying to create the illusion of something that really happened —in this book. I think it can properly be called not a novel but an history. And while its form is very tight, it is my intention to make it seem to have the formlessness of history. History actually is not formless but a long [view?] and a philosophic turn of mind are necessary to see its pattern. And I would like this book to have that quality.

February 23 [FRIDAY]

This is a sad day at the beginning. There is no telling what kind of a day it will end up. A sadness I can't write down although I know what it comes from. It is Friday. You know I had planned to take Saturdays and Sundays away from manuscript. But I don't know. Maybe it would be good to do a part of a day's work on Saturday. We'll just have to see. Maybe two days off would lose the work rhythm. It is surely something to think about. And the book is really beginning to get and keep its own rhythm. This is good because once all the form of a book gets in your bones, then you can only work on the story and the rest comes right. Don't you think that is so?

Today I am going for a haircut. I can hear you gasp. It is nearly two months since I have had one and I think it is about time. I have a mane growing down over my shoulders.

You know I always smoke a pipe when I work—at least I used to and now I have taken it up again. It is strange—as soon as a pipe begins to taste good, cigarettes become tasteless. I find I smoke fewer and fewer cigarettes. Maybe I can cut them out entirely for a while. This would be a very good thing. Even with this little change, my deep-seated and perennial cigarette cough is going away. A few months without that would be a real relief.

Still my pictures and books have not come from Pacific

Grove. They have been over a month on the way. I would be glad if they would arrive. Now the sadness is going away. It was like the little gauzy mists which hang close down to the water in the spring. And when they rise, you hardly know they are gone. Now I have forgotten what the sadness was although I remember the form and feeling of it. How odd—that sadness can turn to gold. Can it be that it is a pleasurable feeling? It might well be.

I must go and have my eyes tested. I am not sure I need a change but it might be. And I sit many hours over this book. It would be just as well if I did it under the best circumstances. Don't you think this? Now to work. It is time and I am getting an early start for I got up early.

Now it is much later in the day. And my work was the longest so far. It is moving at a very rapid pace but everything about it indicates to me that it is going to be a very long book indeed. I know that because every facet I open leads down a long road of character and its effect. Lord this is a complicated book. I hope I can keep all the reins in my hands and at the same time make it sound as though the book were almost accidental. That is going to be hard to do but it must be done. Also I'll have to lead into the story so gradually that my reader will not know what is happening to him until he is caught. That is the reason for the casual—even almost flippant—sound, Pat. It's like a man setting a trap for a fox and pretending with pantomime that he doesn't know there is a fox or a trap in the country. I went to work so early this morning that it is still early. And I could go on and do some more work. But I think the energy core is kind of worn down. I think, since I have done so much so far, that I will let it go for the day. I don't want to get too tired. I want to take enough time so that I will avoid the rather terrible exhaustion of the Grapes of Wrath. I'll tell you one thing though—although this book is more subtle and perhaps less emotional in an obvious way, it is going to be more peopled than the Grapes. We are going to meet—try to know and move on from—one hell of a lot of people. Since in these work notes I am putting down everything freely, I can give you an example of what I mean when I say the book is really beginning to move and breathe and have a life of its own. I had thought to set Carl Trask* and his wife in perhaps three paragraphs. But then I got fascinated with him, not only as a character but with

---

* Charles Trask in the novel. See page 27.

his character as a mover and shaper even if in reverse so that his effect comes moving down the generations. I thought he was going to have only one wife and I find he has two. I thought he was an only child and he has a half brother. I thought to bring him right into the Salinas Valley and now I doubt whether he will get there in under twenty-five pages. I guess that's what I mean by the book taking its own pace and almost thinking for itself.

Now I get the old-old fear and rush—I hope I may live to finish this book. And that will be a long enough life for me. Now that I am in it I cannot see beyond it and increasingly it becomes difficult for me to see out of it. That is the ideal I guess but it doesn't leave much room for thinking for and about one's self. And maybe that is good or maybe it is bad. And now I am going to stop for the day.

February 26 [MONDAY]

Well, there was a party Saturday night and I had a good time. Sorry to break the writing rhythm but I must take some time off or I would soon poison on the script. I know you understand this. I am not too bright this morning but I will start the week just the same. I don't suppose writing consists in anything more than doing it. I am breaking pencil points today—over-vehemence. This is usually the thing that happens at first before a connection establishes. But there isn't any doubt that I will get my day's work done. I am sure of that whether or not it be good. This is not a morning of great joy for some reason or other. I don't understand why some days are wide open and others closed off, some days smile and others have thin slitted eyes and others still are days which worry. And it does not seem to be me but the day itself. It has a nature of its own quite separate from all other days. And this is one of mild worry—not about anything. It goes casting about for something for worry. It can always settle on money and usually does. It is a little difficult this morning. The plumber is here. Doorbell ringing, Louise not here yet and Elaine still asleep. I hate to wake her up because she may have read late but on the other hand if this goes on too long I shall certainly awaken her. I don't like to tramp up and down the steps so often. I have so many little things in my mind this morning. I guess this is one of the difficulties with losing the two week-end days. At first anyway, the concentration goes. I hope to pick it up. And I will. Today am going on with Carl Trask. His life and experience are pretty interesting to me. And surely he is not any different from many people I know. I wonder whether this quick treatment of people is good. Well, it just has to be because this is the way I am going to do it willy or nilly.

You should be glad, for the book now is the important thing. The story stays in back of everything else. No matter what I do, the story is always there—waiting and working kind of like a fermenting mash out of which whiskey will be made eventually but meanwhile the mass bubbles and works and makes foam. And it is very interesting but the product that is wished for—devoutly to be wished for—is the whiskey. All the turmoil and boiling is of no interest to anyone.

From now on, since finally mss. pages are jumping ahead, I will put this work letter opposite the day's work opening.

Now I have done part of this day's work. And the speed of composition increases; I have no idea of the quality. But one thing I must say to you. As I go on, my happiness increases. That is a very odd thing to say but it is true. A kind of joy comes over me. The work I am doing now is observational and evaluative. It may be dull. I need it for my theme and for my story. This is an old-fashioned novel, Pat. It will achieve any effect it has by accumulation rather than by quick and flashing periods. And don't forget that it is going on for hundreds of pages. I only hope it is not dull. But if it should happen to be, then that is the way it is too. Because as I have said before, this book is going to take its own pace. I am going to direct it but not push it about. This is my big novel. I'm going to use every bit of technique I have learned consciously and I am also going to let it go unconsciously—you will see if there is anything to see.

Now this day's work is done. You are going to California tomorrow. That will be so long ago when you read this. And you are coming for coffee this afternoon. Well, we will see. All I know is that little by little it will mount and grow slowly until finally it is a house and then it will either be a good house and will stand or a bad house and then it will fall of its own weight. This is always true both of books and houses. And so the end of today's work. I always am a little sad when a day's work is done.

February 27 [TUESDAY]

This is my birthday. I had intended to work but some things very important came up and I did not. But in the evening went to see Gielgud and Pamela Brown in The Lady's Not for Burning. We found it delightful and delightfully acted. I don't know what the play is about. I suspect nothing but it sounds so pretty.[. . .] Last night I thought of the possibility of getting the boys and I could not sleep. So now I have had about two hours' sleep in two nights and I must say, it doesn't seem to hurt me at all. It's so funny.

February 28 [WEDNESDAY]

Got up early, still without much if any sleep. I haven't time to sleep. Too many things are happening inside me and outside me. And I just haven't the time. Today I have to go to a stock-holders meeting of the ill-fated World Video at 2 P.M. So I am up early to do my work before that time.[. . .] And now to work. It is the boyhood of Adam.

March 1 [THURSDAY]

And snowing heavily. This is a lion March. Yesterday I did not get much done. I guess my brain was as exhausted as the rest of me. But last night I went to bed early and slept long and feel refreshed today. Tomorrow Tom and John are coming over to spend the night. I haven't seen them for a very long time. And I would like to. Also I will get to know them quite a bit better.[. . .] A card from you today, Pat, in flight toward San Francisco. I hope you are having a good time. Now the time has come to go to work. After the little layoff, it is hard.

Now I have finished that day's work. And now I'll make a bookcase.

March 2, Friday

Quite early to work today, Pat. The reason is not far to find. I am going over to get the boys this afternoon and they are going to spend the night with us. And I want to get in a day's work first or a reasonable compromise with a day's work. It is a brilliant sunny day. Really a spring day. But I have to get the work in. I think I know exactly what my scenes are now so there's no point in worrying about time. Waverly* overslept this morning. But fortunately I am developing a good working habit. I awakened her to go to school. I don't know whether you will like any of the work I am now doing. The things are so tenuous as to be barely apparent and yet so powerful that their effects can last over three generations or perhaps into infinity of time. But the point is that I don't know whether I am making that clear. They are so very delicate. Today is one of excitements. The red rug came for our library. Then it will really be a room. When the chairs and the couch come it will be a room fit for such a king as I. Such excitement as a red rug can cause in a house you wouldn't believe. And now it is really time to go to work.

March 5, Monday

Got up at an early hour today but very sluggish because I seem to have had too much sleep. Almost drugged with it. I guess I just can't take too much sleep. The week end pleasant but I missed the good feeling of work. Last week was not very productive in length but I think all right in quality. I seem to be a little over-vehement with the pencils this morning. Wrote a card to you, Pat, in Hollywood. Seemed strange to be addressing you there. You won't like it much. I am assailed with virtue—a feeling toward virtue but without virtue's self. Define virtue! It is that quality of character which is pleasant and desirable to its owner and which makes him perform acts of which he can be proud and with which he can be pleased. I seem to boil up or fulminate very slowly and it is a shame. I should react with great speed. And perhaps I will one day although by now I don't expect it anymore.

It is always amazing to me how we forget our failures. I guess if we didn't, we could not survive. But perhaps it is no bad thing to take a little time to go back over failures, not to glory in them but just to remind ourselves. In the forgetting it is not vainglory that bothers me but simply that things neglected as not done well slip away as though they never had happened. Last night I turned up so many of them hiding in the brush of my background. It seemed to me that if one kept one's self aware of them, they might possibly never be repeated. I think this is vain thinking but I did it anyway. Now a new week opens. And I am going to attack

---

* Waverly Scott, aged fifteen, Elaine's daughter by her previous marriage, who lived with the Steinbecks.

a weighty problem. It is this way. You establish a diet and you lose a certain amount of weight and then you stop. You are on a plateau. It requires violence to break through it. And there is where I am now. So I will smash it in about four days of very little food and then I can go down a few pounds again until I reach another plateau—then violence again. But I believe it is good to stay on the plateaus for a while to get the system strong for the new attack. Now it is time to go to work again.

Going well today. I am trying to hold it down to 1000 words a day for a while. I have always the tendency to hurry and I don't want to this time. I want this book to be a very slow one. I must not let this book run away from me. The story moves but it must move at its own pace. I had thought to get all of the early story of Adam down in one chapter but I can't. It will have to be split over two chapters. I will get him into the army and then leave him and go back to the Hamiltons, and to discussion. Otherwise it would be too long in one stretch. Also, when Adam comes back from the army, he will be a formed man and it will be the thing I have written the whole thing for. And as I have mentioned before and again and again—a story has a life of its own. It must be allowed to take its own pace. It can't be pushed too much. If it is, the warp shows through and the story is unnatural and unsafe. And this story of mine must be safe. At last I wonder how many events are accidents and how many are created and forced by the natures of the protagonists. To a large extent I lean toward the latter.

Later. Now the day's work is over and the story moves. I hope it does. It seems to. But we will see. The morrow's work if I do enough of it will end the chapter. It will consist in the following: the day, the fight, the second talk with Carl, the night, the visit in the night with Alice. And with that I will end the chapter. Then, after a stretch about the Hamiltons I will go back to Connecticut, the girl, the marriage, and the take-off to California.

March 6, Tuesday

Here we go again. No sleep last night but I feel fine. And I don't even know why I didn't sleep. I was perfectly comfortable. Just couldn't let go of consciousness. Funny thing. But an early start today because sometimes fatigue slows me down. And I want to get a good stretch in today—maybe even finish the chapter—but I put little faith in that. Everything in this book turns out to be larger than I had anticipated. I think I put down the next happenings in a previous note. I'll have to look back and see whether a night of consideration . . . Now, once to the toilet and I will go to work.

And some work done but a little bit slow today as why shouldn't it be. I am completely relaxed with this book—perhaps too much relaxed. We'll only see about that later. It is so strange what one writes down. And curious what one remembers. I suppose one remembers just what he wants to remember for his own safety and his own good. And if this is so, why should I not say it in a book? And I should and I will. Because a book—at least the kind of a book I am writing—should contain everything that seems to me to be true. There are few enough true things in the world. It would be a kind of sin to conceal any of them or to hide their little heads in technique as the squeamishness of not appearing in one's own book. For many years I did not occur in my writing. But this was only apparently true—I was in them every minute. I just didn't seem to be. But in this book I am in it and I don't for a moment pretend not to be.

But it goes very slowly today, very slowly. Sometimes I think I like it better this way. I am really mumbling over the syllables today and sometimes that is good and pleasant. Self-indulgence it truly is though, no matter what I say or anyone says. And do you know, Pat, what the chief reason for my enjoyment of this book is? It is because there is no end. It goes on and on into a kind of infinity. And if a book has no end, it does no good to hurry to get it done. So, although my word rate per day is somewhat higher than I would like it, I still don't get anywhere. And that's the way I am going to keep it. I can see you cursing this attitude because it gives you no time to plan on. But I am still going to try to keep it that way.

And there's that day's work done. I thought I might possibly finish the chapter but there's a good part of another day of work on that. This is a very long chapter but then I guess all of these chapters are going to be long. And I know one thing—this book is not going to hold all of this novel. I doubt whether two of them will, using only every other page. I do that because the left-hand page is hard to write on and so it is only

March 7, Wednesday

I should easily finish this chapter today. There isn't a great deal more of it. Yesterday the symbolic killing of brother by brother. I have only the recruiting and the last night with Alice visiting perhaps. But I have other things too. I want to wind this first chapter up well. The others are not so clear cut. But I like a chapter to have design of tone, as well as of form. A chapter should be a perfect cell in the whole book and should almost be able to stand alone. If this is done then the breaks we call chapters are not arbitrary but rather articulations which allow the free movement of the story. I think you will find that the theme is beginning to emerge. And it had to take time. It will emerge again and again. But this time it will just peer out and withdraw. This long-range letter has a curious effect on me. I have the impression that you have already read the earlier ones and I know this is not so. The gifts of Cain and Abel to their father and his rejection of one and acceptance of the other will I think mean a great deal to you but I wonder if it will be generally understood by other readers. We will have to see.

March 8, Thursday

Now, Pat, we come back into the Salinas Valley and to the boys. And this will be the first test of the book's form because it will be the first repetition of a method. You see the first time it is a kind of a surprise. Then the next time there should be recognition and after that the form should seem so natural that you cannot imagine its being done any other way. I hope you liked the ending of Chapter II.*I think it is kind of terrible in a way. And now I go back to the Hamiltons and to my boys. And it is peculiar that I go back to the boys on this particular day. Gwyn called me yesterday to tell me that Tom is refusing to go to school, fights to stay away, claims he misses the bus. When the two of them stayed overnight with me last week I knew that Tom was in some deep emotional trouble, I could feel it. And I am pretty sure it is a simple feeling of rejection, of *not* being loved. [. . .] I'm going to take him into the country Saturday and Sunday to see if I can help him. I'll want to talk to him but mostly I'll want him to talk if I

---

* Chapter 4.

can get him to—and without his brother. I feel that the competition there is so much too great for him under whatever handicaps he feels he has. So you see, coming back in the book to the boys is almost like talking to him in trouble. I guess it is almost time to have some of this book typed up. Jean Ainsworth* offered to do it for me. She says she can read my writing. And of course in this draft it doesn't make a great deal of difference if there are words she can't read. It will be only a correction draft. The story will move along but it will never move quickly. I don't want it to. It has a long slow pace and I will do anything to keep it that way. You will be back from your western trip in about two weeks, and if I can continue at the rate I am going and do not have any accidents that take up time I should have somewhere near a hundred typewritten pages done. I'm not sure of course but I should have nearly sixty done now, but there is no way of telling. I think there are about 2½ pages to the page of my writing unless there is lots of dialogue, in which case it will be 3 pages to the page. But so far there is not a great deal of dialogue except in spots. Of course that will increase as the book goes on. You know as well as I do that this book is going to catch the same kind of hell that all the others did and for the same reasons. It will not be what anyone expects and so the expecters will not like it. And until it gets to people who don't expect anything and are just willing to go along with the story, no one is likely to like this book. It is really time I went to work.

March 12, Monday

Now a new week. We spent the week end at Meredith's † in the country. A quiet time, windy and cold but good. We took Tom with us who Gwyn thought needed a lecture about going to school. He needs more than that. He needs infinite patience and discipline. Elaine gave him lessons and did wonders with him. His blocs would disappear quickly under better conditions. Now a new week of work starts. I hope to God it will be a good one. I have the Hamilton chapter but all tied up with the transition of the Trasks. And in case you have not discovered it, this device gives me the possibility of describing, interpolating, explaining, etc., without seeming to be a bore. Maybe I will be, but I will try not to be. It must be relaxed and easy and at the same time comfortable. As

---

* One of Steinbeck's nieces.
† Burgess Meredith, the actor and director.

always, people in a book change. Thus I am forced to change the name of Carl Trask and for reasons I don't want to tell right now. He has changed his symbolic nature to a certain extent, I guess that is the main reason. And I want the book to be as perfect as possible but it should have some of the imperfections of its subject —namely mankind. Of course there will be others but insofar as it is possible I should like the faults to fit the subjects like the iron tires of a wheel—shrunk on and permanent. Do you know how this is done, Pat? You should know I guess. And maybe I will tell you. Maybe not. It depends on whether the book requires it. Now I have put enough on this page and I will go back to my story and see what I can do with it. Anyway it is surely time for that.

Now—I have concluded a difficult part which is to throw in history and make it sound like conversation and to mingle with this some kind of understanding of the people involved, at least to pose the problem of these people. And further, since these people are essentially symbol people, I must make them doubly understandable as people apart from their symbols. A symbol is usually a kind of part of an equation—it is one part or facet chosen to illuminate as well as to illustrate the whole. The symbol is never the whole. It is a kind of psychological sign language. But in this book, which I want to have a semblance of real experience both visual and emotional and finally intellectual, I want to clothe my symbol people in the trappings of experience so that the symbol is discernible but not overwhelming. So I am nearly done with the transition of Adam Trask but I want to put down one clincher in the form of a letter.

There another day's work done. I hope you will like it. It has much hidden in it.

March 13, Tuesday

Things do happen and continue to happen on the outside. Isn't that odd that I now regard the book as the inside and the world as the outside. And just as long as that is so the book is firm and the outside cannot hurt it or stop it. And I must be sure that it remains that way by never letting time go by without working on it. For it is one thing to have in one's mind that the book will never be done and quite another to let it stop moving. Yesterday it went a little too fast. Today maybe a little too slow, but that is completely unimportant if only it moves a little every day. I have been and have intended to take Saturday and Sunday off for rest and a change of pace and I am not sure I am right. I think from now on I will do something on Saturday, if it is only a paragraph. Two days is too long to be away from it. One day is all right. So I really think I will try that. Even one paragraph is association and it is better. But I will try it and see.

The letter* written by Charles to Adam is a very tricky one and it has in it, concealed but certainly there, a number of keys. I recommend that you read it very carefully—very carefully because if you miss this, you will miss a great deal of this book and maybe will not pick it up until much later. I don't know why I tell you this though, for I am sure you will read it all with great care, as great care as I use in writing it. Sometimes maybe too much care. But I guess that is impossible. And I suppose the subtleties are sooner or later picked out but never by critics.

March 14, Wednesday

I didn't get much done yesterday and probably won't today. Outside things are cutting in. This is bound to happen sometimes. That's why I must take so much time with this book so that I can bridge such days as this. What the outside things are is no part of this record. I must get into the book again at least to try even though my mind is badly cut up in all directions. Very hard to concentrate today. But I must try for my own safety. Take things in stride and particularly don't anticipate trouble before it happens. One of my very worst habits is the anticipation of difficulties and vicariously to go through them in advance. Then, if they happen I have to do it twice, and if they don't happen I have done them unnecessarily. I know this is my habit. Last summer Marge Benchley † drew my attention to this tendency and its futility and Elaine has many times since. But not to do it requires constant watchfulness on my part. I have the recurring tendency. I guess I am what is called a worrier.

Today I had a report that you had seen young Ed Ricketts ‡ in S.F. and talked with him. If I can find your itinerary, I will

---

* At the end of Chapter 4 in the novel.
† Mrs. Nathaniel Benchley.
‡ Son of Steinbeck's marine-biologist friend in Pacific Grove, California, "Doc" in *Cannery Row*. Steinbeck and Ricketts Senior had gone on an expedition together in the Gulf of California which resulted in their collaboration on *Sea of Cortez* (1941).

write you a card. Yes I found it and you will be leaving Hollywood tomorrow so I will write you a card to the Palmer House in Chicago and it may be there when you arrive.

March 15, Thursday

Well I got up early this morning in spite of the fact that I was up until 2:30 laying the hall rug. It was very hard because I was sleepy. But gradually I came out of it. The outside things I spoke of are removed now and I wanted to dip deeply into the work and I have too and now my day's work is done.

There is only one trouble with a story like this which moves of itself. In the light of what happens you have to go back and correct or change so that the two match. This is a very headstrong story, Pat. It has taken its head and it goes as it wishes and I learn from it rather than being taught by it. I shall be interested when you read some of it to know whether you find it slow in the sense of boring. Slow in pace it certainly is. And now I am going to finish some work downstairs and maybe take a walk. You get into Chicago today I guess.

March 16, Friday

I wouldn't say this has been a very good week but I do the best I can. And the book does move along little by little. And it never moves back, that's one thing about it. It lacks tension and that is just exactly what I want and intend it to do. But it may cause trouble to you as a publisher because people have grown to expect tautness and constant action. It's like in the present-day theatre. If there isn't shouting and jumping around it isn't liked. For people seem to have lost the gift for listening. Maybe they never had it. Who knows. The admired books now were by no means the admired books of their day. I believe that Moby Dick, so much admired now, did not sell its first small first edition in ten years. And it will be worse than that with this book. It will be considered old-fashioned and old hat. And to a large extent it is —you have to look closely to see its innovations even though there are many. And in pace it is much more like Fielding than like Hemingway. I don't think the lovers of Hemingway will love this book. You may have noticed that young people in particular like only one kind of book. They cannot enlarge to like more than one. I myself have been guilty of this.

The week end comes on. To me it has been a very short week. So much has happened outside of the book, things that could not be helped. I hope that next week may not have so many things. They tend to confuse me out of all proportion. We go to the theatre tonight and Waverly is giving a party for thousands of teen-agers. Just as well we are going to the theatre I guess, and besides, the kids don't want us around any more than we want to be.

March is the month my mother was really afraid of. She practically held her breath until it was over every year. For every-thing bad happened to our family in March. But she herself I believe lived through March and died in April. But all her life she hated March. I don't think this is unusual. March is a nervous month, neither winter nor spring and the winds make people nervous.

Now it is time for me to go to work.

March 19, Monday

Well it was a big week end. Waverly had a big party on Friday—about twenty-five kids—and nine girls stayed all night. They were very good, however, and there was no trouble. We went to see The Rose Tattoo and liked it very well. I have a real uncom-fortable stomach upset. Kind of biliousness. It will go away but hard to ignore because I feel lousy. Today I have to work on this book and then rework the last scene of Zapata* so I do wish I felt better. Annie Laurie* comes out of the hospital today. I was going down to see her—but too much work. I can't.

Had cards from you and from Dorothy † today. But you must have been in Chicago for some days. I think you are due home tomorrow or maybe today. I don't know how much invention my stomach-bitten mind has today but I will do the best I can. And that's all I can ever do. Still on the Hamiltons and will be for several days but I should get the third chapter ‡ done sometime this week. My head is really spinning today. I hope I don't have that intesti-nal flu that is so prevalent. I've been lucky for a long time. Haven't been sick in a very long time. And I would like to keep it

---

* Steinbeck had been commissioned to write a film script on the life of Emiliano Zapata, the Mexican revolutionist. Annie Laurie Williams, associated with McIntosh and Otis, was his agent for film and stage rights on all his work.
† Mrs. Pascal Covici.
‡ Chapter 5.

that way. But I am surely having some violent symptoms today. But little by little they will leave, I am sure. They always do. I have had a fine unbroken record of good health for which I am grateful.

Now back to the book. You will have noticed I am sure that I am trying by a slow leisurely pyramiding of detail to give an impression not so much of the physical life of the county as of the kind of spiritual life—the thinking life—the state of mind—the plateau of tho\`ght. As we go along there will be more of the physical life. But I think it fairly important that I give a kind of mood of the Valley. What do you think?

March 20, Tuesday

As I think I remarked yesterday, you should be back from Chicago today, but maybe you are staying on. Who knows. I think you'll call me when you do.

I feel a little slump today. But I should not mind. There have been precious few of those in this book. I have been very lucky in this book in having so few. Very lucky. I must expect many more but I am so happy that the work doesn't seem to be such a struggle.

I think you will recognise that the Hamilton sections are much more difficult than the Trask sections. For the Trask chapters flow along in chronological story while the Hamilton chapters which play counterpoint are put together with millions of little pieces, matched and discarded. Also I am playing all around in time with the Hamilton sections. By this method I hope to get over a kind of veracity which would be impossible with straight-line narrative. But oh! Jesus am I going to catch critical hell for it. My carefully worked out method will be jumped on by the not too careful critic as slipshod. For it is not an easy form to come on quickly nor to understand immediately. As I have said before, this is not a new nor an old-fashioned book but my culling of all books plus my own invention. Now for some white-magical reason, my slump is gone—

History—a new department, daily to synchronize the writing of this book with the other world which sometimes becomes a little unreal. The Kefauver Committee has been hearing witnesses regarding govt. and crime. Showing on television and very popular. Yesterday ex-mayor, now Ambassador O'Dwyer testified. The whole thing a kind of fairy dance. Everybody lying and everybody knowing everyone is lying. A few minor officials will be hurt. This morning the Schuman Plan started its route for signature. This, I think is the beginning of the pattern of the future—the opening of the supra-state. Our businessmen in particular and people in general are very much in fear of communism. Now mark my prophecy —The so-called communist system will break up and destroy itself in horrible civil wars because it is not a permanent workable system. It will fly apart from its own flaws. On the other hand the Schuman Plan is a workable system. The businessmen so anxious about the status quo have little to fear from communism. The Schuman Plan is the thing that will change the world. I do not believe that America can compete with this new form of sponsored and controlled cartel. We will be forced either to fight it or to join it, and if we join it world govt. will be established. If we fight it, we will lose. It has always been my contention that political world govt. will only follow economic world govt. and that laggingly. The United Nations tries to reverse the process and I do not believe that is possible. (End of prediction.) Next— There are indications that the Soviet state and its satellites are having some kind of internal trouble. This should be the time when we should help out with that by making or pretending to make deals with dissidents. Here, Pat, is I think our one danger of war. If the Soviet Union is in reasonably good shape, she will *not* go to war now and will try to avoid it always. *But* if the regime in the Kremlin is in danger it might well enter a war to preserve itself even though that process might be its destruction. And that should hold you for a while. Of time and space and the eye to see and the ear to hear and also of the tongue to speak. And what is that—a person set off, set aside and up or down.

March 21, Wednesday

Dear Pat: It is the first day of spring and you aren't back yet. At least you haven't phoned. Today is packing day for Way.* She goes out tonight to California. I hope to get a lot done on my book. But I can truthfully say that I am satisfied with the progress of the book in the time I have been working. I do from five to seven typed pages a day and there are few days when I have missed. I want it to be this slow. I want it to take a year to write. I noticed an announcement that Viking hoped to get it in the fall.

---

* Waverly Scott.

This is not going to happen. There is too much of it. I have 35 handwritten pages, probably 90 typed pages. And I will surely cross the first hundred pages this week. But this means nothing to a book that is going to be six or seven hundred pages long. It is the very bare beginning. Jean Ainsworth is going to start typing next week on draft. Now that is another reason the book is going to take long: it is going to be much more carefully rewritten than anything I have ever done. This book is very important to me. I am going to do no going back until the whole is completed but then it is going to be overhauled very very deeply. I shall insist on that. This is my big book. And it has to be a big book, and because it is new in form although old in pace it has to be excellent in every detail. And I don't care how long it takes to make it that way and I mean this. You can't train for something all your life and then have it fall short because you are hurrying to get it finished. So there. Meanwhile you had better be shopping around for another book for me to write in because this one is only going to last about two more months due to the fact that I only use every other page. I judge that this book will have in it roughly 110 thousand words of book or perhaps half of the book. That is my idea of it anyway. With slips that will take about sixty working days and of course there are bound to be days lost besides the week ends. So I rather think, barring accidents, by the first of July I shall have half the book done. It is strange to talk in these figures. I myself don't care when I get half the book done. I am just telling it to you as the present rate of progress. That may speed or slow. I don't know which. But by the first of July, you'd better have a new book for me. You must think I waste an awful lot of time on these notes to you but actually it is the warm-up period. It is the time of drawing thoughts together and I don't resent it one bit. I apparently have to dawdle a certain amount before I go to work. Also if I keep the dawdling in this form I never leave my story. If I wrote my dawdles some other way I would be thinking all over the map. My mind is very restless and it leaps like a grasshopper. And so I keep it that way. A good part of my day's work is laid out. And it goes in my boys' chapter and it refers to the ending of the century and the coming into the new. It is a thing I have thought a great deal about and I am going to try to put it down as a mood more than any other way. I think it should have its own chapter but since I want to keep the alternate qualities I think I will make it a subhead chapter under III. That way I will keep the things well separated.

And now it is time for me to get to it. I called your office and you have not come back yet. Where the hell are you?

Still March 21, Wednesday

Well that was a tough one. I hope it is good. I really do. God knows it is different. And it is concentrated. I said I was going to plant it with emotion. I don't know whether or not I have. How can I know. I haven't read it to anyone yet. Maybe tomorrow I will read it to Elaine. She will know. I'm trying to implant a counterpoint of poetry just before the harsh prose that has to follow. I want always balances in this book—must have them. And that is all for this day.

March 22, Thursday

Well you are home on the same day that I start on my chapter four.* And you say that you are coming over this afternoon. That is good. I'll be very glad to see you. Last night I read the Hamilton chapter and the transition b and c to Elaine and she said she liked them very well. I hope you will. They are odd and maybe a little indigestible maybe to some but it has to be that way. Just has to. And now, Pat, I am going into the fourth chapter. You know, I just looked up and saw how different my handwriting is from day to day. I think I am writing much faster today than I did yesterday. That gives a sharpness to the letter. And also I have found a new kind of pencil—the best I have ever had. Of course it costs three times as much too but it is black and soft but doesn't break off. I think I will always use these. They are called Blackwings and they really glide over the paper. And brother, they have some gliding to do before I am finished. Now to the work.

In Chapter IV I go back to Connecticut and the Trasks. It is a very long chapter—like most of them almost a novelette. And it has in it a number of facets and a great many images. Roughly, here is what happens. Adam goes home. His father has died at exactly the time he was demobilised. The father has left money, $20,000, and there was no way for him to have got the money. With $10,000 apiece the brothers are rich for those days. Charles is married by this time to a girl named Amy. Then we have the episode of the girl coming to the house at night. Adam falls in love

* This, much changed, developed into Chapters 6 through 11.

34

with her in spite of every warning including her own. He simply does not listen. He asks her to marry him. Charles warns him and, when he insists, offers to buy his part of the farm. Adam refuses and we have the frightfulness of Adam being driven out. And that is the way he is started on his way to California. You will notice also the change from large chunks of time to minute treatments. I may have to find divisions within chapters to take the place of time and scene changes, but there are simple mechanical things which are not hard to do or to imagine. But now to the work and we will see how it goes.

March 23, Good Friday

You are coming over today to watch us dye Easter eggs. It is a funny business, yesterday I felt the work was going to be very easy. And do you know, it was six thirty in the evening before I had done what I wanted. The fact of the matter is that you just cannot tell how anything is going to work or how hard or easy it will be. It always fools you. Today I am under a sense of some rush. Going to quit early and go up to get the boys. And I hate to rush except that I have to. Going to Long Island tomorrow to stay the night. But I'll take this book along just in case.

I hope the incident of the scarred forehead does not throw you. It is going to be a kind of a recurring symbol in various forms. And what does it mean? Oh I could tell you, the maimed, the marked, the guilty—all such things, the imperfect. It is a haunting thing. But there are a great many haunting things in this book. Today I want to get Adam home if I can, and I can.

You know I am really stupid. For years I have looked for the perfect pencil. I have found very good ones but never the perfect one. And all the time it was not the pencils but me. A pencil that is all right some days is no good another day. For example, yesterday, I used a special pencil soft and fine and it floated over the paper just wonderfully. So this morning I try the same kind. And they crack on me. Points break and all hell is let loose. This is the day when I am stabbing the paper. So today I need a harder pencil at least for a while. I am using some that are numbered 2⅜. I have my plastic tray you know and in it three kinds of pencils for hard writing days and soft writing days. Only sometimes it changes in the middle of the day, but at least I am equipped for it. I have also some super soft pencils which I do not use very often because I must feel as delicate as a rose petal to use them. And I

35

am not often that way. But when I do have such moments I am prepared. It is always well to be prepared. Pencils are a great expense to me and I hope you know it. I buy them four dozen at a time. When in my normal writing position the metal of the pencil eraser touches my hand, I retire that pencil. Then Tom and Catbird get them. And they need pencils. They need lots of pencils. Then I have this kind of pencil and it is too soft. ★ Whenever you see a thing like that, the point broke. I have fine prejudices, lazy ones and enjoyable ones. It occurs to me that everyone likes or wants to be an eccentric and this is my eccentricity, my pencil trifling. It isn't a very harmful one. Maybe I have others which are more. The electric pencil sharpener may seem a needless expense and yet I have never had anything that I used more and was more help to me. To sharpen the number of pencils I use every day, I don't know how many but at least sixty, by a hand sharpener would not only take too long but would tire my hand out. I like to sharpen them all at once and then I never have to do it again that day. So, you will say, I have wasted enough time for one day but I have managed to do something else too. I have lost the sense of rush with which I started this and that is exactly what I intended to do.

Still March 23, still Good Friday

I am only going to do one page today. Of course it will be more than the usual in typescript because there is a good deal of dialogue. But I have to go and get the boys now and buy Easter egg dyes and candies to make them sick. As a matter of fact you are coming over this afternoon. I'm not going to read any of this to you but you can look through it all you like. And at any time too. I know it is rough and will need lots of rewriting but I am never shy about it when a professional is doing the reading. But God save me from amateurs. They don't know what they are reading but it is much more serious than that. They immediately start rewriting. I never knew this to fail. It is invariable. For that matter, I think I dislike amateurs in any field. They have the authority of ignorance and that is something you simply cannot combat. It is just about time for me to discontinue the work for today and I kind of don't want to because some very exciting things are coming. Maybe I can do some tonight after everyone is gone and the house is quiet.

March 24, Saturday

Well you came here yesterday. As you know, I was determined not to read to you but when I saw you struggling with your
magnifying glass, I couldn't help myself. I did try to read a little.
And you said you liked what you heard. Now it is Saturday.
Normally I would not work but I got up at 6:30 mainly because
I had had enough sleep. Also, yesterday I had to stop in the
middle of a scene. I would like to follow through with the relationship of the brothers. And also another discovery. I wonder what
the effect of that would be. I'll have to see. But I really would like
to see what will happen if these two young men are confronted
with a reversal of everything they believed. It would have a great
impact, a frightening impact. However, we will see.

Still March 24, Saturday

Well I got my full quota done. And it's another change of
pace. And I hope you like it and I'll bet there are some few surprises in it for you, but you'll find it all planted earlier.

March 26, Monday

New week and I think March is a very long month. This year
it seems longer than any I can remember. I wonder why that is.
The last couple of days I have gone into a deep slump. Natural I
guess. One can't always be on top of the world. Oddly enough the
slump in spirit has not stopped the book at all which by now
seems to have an independent existence. Now it is Monday and a
new week starting. My slump over this week end was so great that
I thought I was sick. But no. Just my manic depressiveness coming
out in me. Maybe I will telephone you today. I wonder whether
what I read to you stays with you. Elizabeth* says it does with
her. Just talked to you and you say it does also. I hope this
continues. I am particularly fascinated with Adam's reaction to
the death and defection of his father. That will go down hard with
you and with everyone else. It did at first with me but once you
have accepted it, you will see that it is righter than any conventional
approach could be. In fact his reaction I think is most profound.
And you will be interested to know that Adam made it himself.
I did not do it for him. There is nothing unusual in the fact that

---

* Elizabeth Otis, his long-time literary agent, friend, and confidante.

he who did not like his father nevertheless had faith in him. You and even I must think a good deal about that because in it lies one of the great truths. When you look at it you will see that love is identification and embodies jealousy and suspicion. Think of that. Faith is an entirely different thing. Love can only weaken faith. Consider this in a world spirit. We suspect our own govt., which we love, of every kind of lie and chicanery. On the other hand we as a people find ourselves believing and having faith in everything the Kremlin says. Isn't that interesting? The propaganda of our enemy always seems much more true than our own.

This is going to be a big week of work. I feel that surely. I have perhaps to get Adam moved to California by the end of the week.

I wonder why, on such a day as this, when the story is particularly clear in my head, I have a kind of virginal reluctance to get to it. I seem to want to think about it and moon about it for a very long time before I actually get down to it. Today, I think I know one of the main reasons. Today's work is so important that I am afraid of it. It requires the use of the most subtle rhythms both of speech and thought. And I use that last advisedly because thought has its rhythms and qualities just as poetry has. I think that the two are very closely related. Thus after a couple of days off, I think I write in this page almost like a pitcher warming up to pitch—getting my mental arm in shape to pitch a good game. And the pitcher is not a bad symbol since he must have smoothness and coordination and rhythm all together.

One more section and then I am through with this. I dislike thinking of myself as different or set aside or separate from other people and yet I am forced to sometimes, much as I dislike it. It is borne in upon me that I do not like the pastimes which amuse and satisfy others—the games, both mental and physical, cards, gambling, tennis, croquet. It is not that I dislike them but that they bore me and in no way hold my attention. This is a matter of sadness to me because I want to like them just as I want to like all foods. But there is no answer to this. I just do not find anything to interest me in them. And now that is enough.

March 26, Monday, continued

Well—there I got that premise down in dialogue.* And since this is one of the very most important things in the book, it

---

* Chapter 7 [3].

is my hope that it comes over clearly. This must be remembered because on this rests a large part of my structure of the book. The relationship between the brothers has now been finally established and established finally, but unless it is clear, it is gibberish. But isn't it exciting? Aren't they really living people? This is the time when I am glad I am or try to be a writer—the growth and flowering of something I seem only to plant and nurture for a while. You will wonder what is going to happen next and I am not going to tell you. I'm going to make it a surprise to you. I will tell you this though— After a transitional section a new relationship comes in and it is on the basis of this that Adam goes to California. And I don't know how long it will be because now I have to build a whole new person right from the ground. This is a woman and you must know her; know her completely because she is a tremendously powerful force in the book. And her name is Catherine or Cathy— Does that give you any clue to her?

March 27, Tuesday

Today I have a transition of the brothers and then I go to Cathy. And Cathy is a hustler, perhaps born, perhaps caused by accident but Cathy is by nature a whore. She also is by profession a whore. Why Adam Trask should have fallen in love with her is anybody's guess but I think it was because he himself was trained to operate best under a harsh master and simply transferred that to a tough mistress. She is quite a girl and I think I will have to go back and develop her at least a little so that what she does later is believable.

Last night I read the last scene to Elaine and she said she liked it. The love as opposed to faith, she said, was very clearly stated and clear. You see, Pat, I don't care about being agreed with on this but I do want it to be understood before the suffering happens. Now I wonder whether you have been getting a sense of the men as people in this book. This is rather important, because in this book people dominate the land, gradually. They strip it and rob it. Then they are forced to try to replace what they have taken out. I am going to subscribe to the Salinas paper again. It would be good to start it coming. But I've forgotten the man's name. It is probably in my file. Well I found it and sent off the letter.

Today is a dawdly day. They seem to alternate. I do a whole of a day's work and then the next day, flushed with triumph, I dawdle. That's today. The crazy thing is that I get about the same number of words down either way. This morning I am clutching the pencil very tight and this is not a good thing. It means I am not relaxed. And in this book I want to be just as relaxed as possible. Maybe that is another reason I am dawdling. I want that calmness to settle on me that feels so good—almost like a robe of cashmere it feels. And gradually it will come as I write this page. That is what is so wonderful about having all year for this book. If I could not relax today I would not write. I would sit over this book for the usual number of hours but I would not write down any of the story for fear it might carry my own tension.

Today is a day of little interruptions. And I have a theory about this. I think we call such things down on ourselves. Interruptions seem to come only on dawdly days. Then the phone rings and the doorbell and packages arrive. And I can't hold still when a package is delivered. I *have* to know what it is. There is no way out of that.

Now I think I am almost ready for the day's work. Incidentally, your enthusiasm for this book is a great stimulant to me. I know how badly you want it to be good. And you can believe truly that I want it to be good much more than you do. So I will get to it now.

March 27, *continued*

There I finished that—a message to Tom and John, and to the general reader, which sounds like a small thing and really is a kind of instruction in how to think about this book and in a sense how to think about the life and the people around them. I intended to make it sound guileless and rather sweet but you will see in it the little blades of social criticism without which no book is worth a fart in hell. I think it was a good day's work. I really do. I am pleased with it in several directions for it does these things or tries to—it seems as a transition from one kind of life to another. It quite honestly tells its purpose and explains the purpose of the new character. And finally it chops off stupid criticism before it can happen. I think it is well said and at the same time disarming. By addressing it to the boys,* it allows a superficial reader to escape its implications if he wishes. So there it is. And tomorrow I go into a new and to me a fascinating character.

---

* Chapter 8. See footnote on page 7.

Now—I think I must go for an eye test very soon because it seems to me that I get tired in the whole region about my eyes. And this might be because my eyes are needing an adjustment in glasses. I sit here too long to take the chance. So maybe next week I will go because I want to take Tom with me too and have his eyes tested. If I do it first, it will remove any uneasiness from him. If there is nothing wrong with his eyes it does no harm. But if he does have eye trouble, he would not know it, and a good many things could be attributed to it. Now I am through for the day and I go to my little works about the house. As Louella Parsons says, "That's all for today. See you tomorrow."

March 28 [WEDNESDAY]

Today—moved by some purposeless perverseness—I don't think I will work. Maybe it is a declaration of some kind of freedom if it should be a kind of freedom I don't want. Now the declaration of freedom is peculiarly pure because it is based neither on laziness nor lack of preparation. I didn't go to sleep early last night so I worked out the next sequence in great detail. And far from being lazy today, I am filled with energy. And it is not based on wanting to do something else because I don't. I am just not going to work today with a period on it. It must mean something to me, but what I do not know. I finished my copper table early this morning. And I think it is very fine. One of my things that I invented that works. Not all do but once in a while one does. The design is plain and fine and it goes with the room. Oh! when the library furniture comes I think I will rarely move out of that room. I don't think I will for that is going to be a balm to my life. My life seems pretty full of balms just now. Say, it's wonderful to declare holiday for no reason. It feels good. But simple holiday is not enough. I'm going to get a haircut this afternoon—a real genuine haircut. And I might go farther and get a little sweet-smelling tonic rubbed on. This is a real festival day for me with garlands. And you, old word-Scrooge, will curse and mutter because I am wasting time. Well, I defy you.

I'll get back to the work a little now. At least in this part. I swear I am not going to write one word in the other. Cathy Ames is a monster—don't think they do not exist. If one can be born with a twisted and deformed face or body, one can surely also come into the world with a malformed soul. All this we will go into in the body of the book. Cathy is important for two reasons.

If she were simply a monster, that would not bring her in. But since she had the most powerful impact on Adam and transmitted her blood to her sons and influenced the generations—she certainly belongs in this book and with some time given to her. There is one thing I don't think any one has ever set down although it is true—to a monster, everyone else is a monster. This I am going into at some length. My god this can be a good book if I can only write it as I can hear it in my mind. This Trask chapter is as dark and dour as a damp tunnel. It has to be. And the next Hamilton chapter is very light and gay. I'll have my contrasts all right. It will be all contrasts and balances. There's nothing wrong with that.

Elaine nearly got a cold but penicillin inhalant seems to have stopped it in its tracks. I surely hope so. I am just about to leave all of this and you and this book until tomorrow. Believe me this is so.

March 29, Thursday

Now one of those rare days when the diary is ahead of the work. I think that will be remedied today though, as of today. I must say I enjoyed my day of rebellion and rest very much. I did many things, redesigned a toilet and rebuilt it, fixed my fish bowl. Looked for a dining room table and went to bed and to sleep very early. Got a wonderful night's sleep. Tonight we go to the opening of the new Rodgers & Hammerstein musical, The King and I. I am sure we will enjoy it although I could wish that these two had more to say and used more. But it will be lovely, I am sure. I put off asking for tickets and only day before yesterday called Morey Jacobs. He is the business manager. He was also Sam Harris's manager. So I have been on two shows with him. He gave us two on the aisle in the fourth row. What a nice thing to do.

It is amazing how many things there are to do in a house, new house or old house. And for some reason I love to make the little repairs and improvements myself. A curious penuriousness comes out in me about paying a man twenty-five dollars for doing badly what I can do just as badly in less time. Besides I can improvise and most people can't. Give me a box of odds and ends of metal and wood and I can build dam near anything. But it isn't only penuriousness either. I love to do it. It gives me some kind of satisfaction. Now I have worked out a way of arranging plants on an old hat rack we bought. I think my method is wonderful but I had to invent it and I don't think anyone else would ever have thought of it. This gives me pleasure, believe it or not. And when that is finished I will have something else to work on. Now—I must stop thinking of my inventions and get back to my book. I have Cathy Ames to present. She is at once a complex and a simple character. It is the custom nowadays in writing to tell nothing about a character but to let him emerge gradually through the story and the dialogue. This is what you might even call the modern fashionable method. But I don't have to do this. Using my method which is neither new nor old-fashioned, I can tell everything I can about a character but not only that, I can analyse and even say what I think about the character. Then if that person also comes through in the action and dialogue, one is pretty far ahead. I am not trying to fool my reader nor to trick him anymore than I would want to fool the little boys to whom this book is ostensibly written. It took three years of puzzled thinking to work out this plan for a book. Believe me, today I am not putting off work. In fact it is nudging me to get to it but I do want to set these things down. In the Bedford Hotel so many centuries [ago] when I was working out the writing plan for this book (remember?) I had thought to restrict my form in an iron cast, to stylize it like an Egyptian wall painting, to give it a language made especially for it and for nothing else. But that was a thousand years and millions of thoughts ago. And finally arrived at the present plan which I am trying to put into effect. Since this book is about everything, it should use every form, every method, every technique. I do not think this will make it obvious because even though I bring most everything to the surface, there will still be the great covered thing. I wonder whether even this far along you have hit on the great covered thing or things. And, Pat, I can't tell my reader that thing because if he knows that pattern in advance, he will start looking for it and will not absorb it. That is why it is concealed. I even hope reviewers do not find it and splash it all around. And that is all for right now.

March 30, Friday

Well, March is nearly over—the month my mother dreaded so is nearly over. Mother never drew a carefree breath in March. All of her tragedies happened in March. And I have noticed that it is an interminable month. It goes on forever. Well, you came over yesterday and picked up the first section of the book to be typed. I wonder what you will think of it in the cold light of print. Hope it does not disappoint you too much. I have just about forty thousand words down or a little less than one quarter I guess. I judge the book is going something over 200,000 words. I have only been on it two months. I think I started Jan. 29. About 8 months more, with luck, will finish it I guess.

Last night went to see the opening of The King and I. It is a very beautiful show about nearly nothing. It will be a great hit. But it just doesn't say anything except one spurious thing. It says that if you fool other people into thinking you aren't afraid then you won't be. And I don't believe that at all. I believe you can only be unafraid if you find out what it is you fear and conquer it. All the pretense in the world won't help you otherwise. At least that's what I believe. It is a thin show which covers its thinness with luxury.

After the theatre we went to Sardi's and had dinner and saw many friends. It is so long since we have been out that it was fun, but somewhere I picked up a great sadness. I think it was from John O'Hara. That is the only thing I can think of which could have caused it. And it has persisted all day today. I have not worked today because I was afraid my book would take on the quality of my sadness. So far I have been singularly free of personal feelings and emotions which can so easily taint a book. I'll work tomorrow and maybe Sunday too so my word rate will keep up. But that is not important.

By the way Cathy had a curious kind of skin—very strange kind of a glow. She is a fascinating and horrible person to me. But there are plenty like her. That I know. Tomorrow I will finish my description of her and get into her terrible story. And it is a terrible story. But there are stories much more terrible and true things more terrible than any story. Now because Cathy's story is so unusual, I must tell it with the greatest casualness as though there were nothing unusual about it. Once you know that Cathy is a monster then nothing she does can be unusual in a monster. You can't go into the mind of a monster because what happens there is completely foreign and might be gibberish. It might only confuse because it would not be rational in an ordinary sense. Cathy has great power over people because she has simplified their weaknesses and has no feeling about their strengths and goodnesses. Don't you know people like that? I almost hesitate to put her down. But you have to believe her. She is just one of the gallery which will move through this book. Lord, what a book—it really moves. Her skin is oil-soaked of course. That is what gives it the pearly light.

Now—only one more thing. Since I know how difficult it is to read my writing under the best circumstances, I shall make a very hard try to write clearly so that it will not be so difficult. That is the least I can do. I will make the effort anyway.

And that is all for today.

April 2, Monday

A book comes in fits and jerks, Pat. Actual wordage on S.V.* started Feb. 15. It made very good progress for quite a long time, in fact until last Thursday. Then you came over and took the first part for typing. Now I don't know whether there is any connection but right then I went into a tail spin. The next three days, through Sunday, I went into a depression that was devastating. I do not think it was because of taking away the mss., but the whole thing is such a delicate matter that I just don't know. What I do know is that it was very painful, hard on me and perhaps harder on Elaine. Now it is Monday and I am all weak and shaken. I am forced to lift myself out of the despondency by the bootstraps. And I will. There is one other thing. Kazan † has found that he cannot make the picture in Mexico. He has gone to Santa Fe to look for locations. It must be made in this country or not at all. Now it also occurs to me that my contract was contingent on this getting the acceptance of the Mexican government. This would void that contract. I don't think Gadg would have moved without talking to Zanuck so maybe that is taken into consideration. Third, our State Department will not take a good view of a picture made in face of opposition from the Mexican govt. It seems that there is no honesty anywhere. And if New York politics seem crooked, they are nothing compared with the expedient politics of Mexico. We will just have to see what happens. I will probably know today.

I think one of the next things I am going to do is to make a new book to hold my papers of this size so that I can write on a single sheet instead of a book which is clumsy. I think I know how to do it but I will have to see. It would be much easier for

---

* "The Salinas Valley" had been the working title from the beginning.
† Elia Kazan ("Gadg") was to be director of the Zapata film. Darryl Zanuck was the producer. It was released under the title *Viva Zapata*.

me I am sure. Anyway that is my next building project. And I
will work it out somehow. Just now I am making a lovely bird
cage. My own design. I design many things and some of them
work, really do. It would be odd if I became known for my designs more than my writing, wouldn't it? I am now designing a
new back to the house. It would be beautiful if I could work it.
And I can. But it will take a lot of building. And I will have to
think about it very carefully. And I can do that too. I can see
it in my head and from that can work it out. If I can only find
some old glass I can do it very well I think. Now I must stop thinking about that entirely. The point is that I like to make the
designs. And I really work some of them out too. Now back to the
book and this time it is permanent. Cathy is going to start emerg-
ing pretty soon now. I hope I can make her believable.

Waverly comes home today from her vacation. The house
will stop being quiet now and will start jumping. And that is
good. It works out fine. When I am working, Waverly and her
friends are at school. They rarely get back before I am finished.
And I love to have them around. Now I must get to Cathy. And
Cathy is going to worry a lot of children and a lot of parents
about their children but I have been perfectly honest about her
and I certainly have her prototype. So here goes.

There—that is the first incident of Cathy's life. There will
be two more before she leaves home and two more before she
meets Adam. I think she will meet Adam this week. Tomorrow I
think I can do both. I went over my day's average today. I think
I may go over it every day this week. I find that after a day or
two of slump I usually do more for a few days. And besides I
want to catch up and I lost some time last week and I may lose
some more this week. Waverly got back and says she is very glad
to be back.

April 3, Tuesday

Waverly came home yesterday and we had a pleasant home-
coming party. She was very tired so as usual Elaine and I stayed
up for her. I guess we just have no sense. But in spite of that I
am up early this morning. Feeling fine. Sometimes I get a little
panicky—so many things I do not do now that I am writing. I
put all the burdens on Elaine, of running the house and doing the
many hundreds of things living entails. So far she hasn't com-

plained. I help with what I can but I am very thoughtless—very. My mind goes mooning away. I never get very far from my book. And this must get pretty tiresome. I'm sure it does. I guess a writer is only half a man as far as a woman is concerned. And Pat, there is so much violence in me. Sometimes I am horrified at the amount of it. It isn't very well concealed either. It lies very close to the surface.

You know I am really a stupid fool. All of these years I have written in a big book because I love the fine paper with lines. But to get the paper I have to take the covers. And I get my wrist burned and very tired after I pass the middle of the page. The rise of an inch makes a very great difference in tiredness. Now after all of these years, it occurs to me that I can just as well take the pages out and write on each sheet separately. Why never before? In this book, which is going to be rebound anyway, I am only now just learning this. It is really stupid of me. However, that's the way it is. I am going to try to write more than my quota today. I can take all day at it so it doesn't matter. I don't think of anything which can interfere with me. Yesterday I ordered a carpenter's workbench for my room. I have always wanted one and never in my life had one. It is a very strange half life I had. I haven't the brains of a mud turtle. And maybe it is a good thing. If I had any brains I would blow them out probably. But I am going to have a little workbench just the same, where I can work with my little tools. I love to do that, I really do. There's a broken chair right now that I really want to get fixed. I had to work out the technique for fixing it because it is the worst broken-up thing you ever saw. Say, I also have to do some rewiring of fixtures in the house. So many things to do. And my pencils are getting short too, very short. I need four dozen new ones. I should get them today. Isn't it a strange luxury I allow myself of using long pencils? When they get so short that the metal around the eraser touches my hand, I give them to Tom or distribute them to Elaine and Waverly because they don't care much about long pencils. On the third finger of my right hand I have a great callus just from using a pencil for so many hours every day. It has become a big lump by now and it doesn't ever go away. Sometimes it is very rough and other times, as today, it is as shiny as glass. It is peculiar how touchy one can become about little things. Pencils must be round. A hexagonal pencil cuts my fingers after a long day. You see I hold a pencil for about six hours every day. This may seem strange but it is true. I am really a conditioned animal with a conditioned hand. And now it is time for me to go back to Cathy. She is going to have several adventures today.

April 4, Wednesday

And now, dear Pat, another day and one of incidents. This is a horrible section of the book but one that is necessary. And I think I want to make it clear that true things quite often do not sound true unless they are made to. Maybe there should be an essay about this. You open the morning paper and you will find a dozen stories of people who have done things which are not true to you because they are not in your experience. Yesterday a grown boy killed both of his parents because they would not let him use the car. You accept that but put it in a story and you would have to use every art to make it acceptable.

This chapter dealing with the background of Cathy is probably one of the longest in the book. The question of length can only arise if it does not hold interest. I think this holds interest. It is just a question of its necessity but as you read along I think you will see that it is all necessary in the light of what is going to happen. I want to have made a kind of suggestive deadliness about this section.

I am at work early today and that is a good thing. I am going to get Tom late this afternoon and bring him home. Tomorrow I will take him for an eye test and incidentally one for me also. I think my eyes need a check. Little headaches are starting on a slight sense of strain. So it is time I guess. I'll keep Tom until Friday. And we will have lessons. He needs lessons. We make it fun and a kind of triumph for him when he wins. Already Gwyn says he is doing better.

Now, with all the fuss about the picture I don't know what we are going to do. If the picture is made in the west and they want me there, what will I do? Take the boys? Kazan now says June 3 is his starting date. But to relax and see what happens. Just get my two pages written every day. That's the best and only thing I can do. Anyway, now the notes are over. And it is time for me to make a couple of calls on the phone and then get to my day's work.

I have just put in a call for you but you are out for coffee. This does not surprise me at all. You are out for coffee a good deal I think.

Well you finally got back from your coffee. I am glad to hear that the typing is going along all right. It will be good to have typescript but I don't intend to look at it for a good time, mainly until I get the whole thing done, so there.

And now the time has come to get back to Cathy.

Well, that is that part. It should have a shivering effect and perhaps it does. Who knows. It went very fast today. But it is generally going fast I think. Now there is a transition scene coming up and I think at the end of the day's work tomorrow Cathy will be ready to meet Adam. This is a brutal chronicle but necessary. It is not a pretty story but I think it has vigor. I think my reader knows and still doesn't know what is going to happen. So tomorrow you will know and, farther than that, you will know what happened after that. That will be the trick. If I can keep the next part casual it will be a triumph because it is the most uncasual story in the world. And the only way to do that well is to make it seem so ordinary that it creeps in on you. That is what I am trying to do with this whole book—to keep it in an extremely low pitch and to let the reader furnish the emotion. If I can do that I will have succeeded. And now that is all for today. I hope you can wait for the next episode. I can hardly wait but my shoulder is sore and my hand is beat up and besides I have come to a natural stopping place. So good-bye.

April 5 [THURSDAY]

I don't know how much I can get done today. Tom is here but Elaine is keeping him downstairs. If I can just get my transition scene done I will be satisfied. Then I can pick it up tomorrow and take Cathy right into Adam's arms. It is a beautiful day. Perfectly lovely. Both Tom and I are going to have our eyes tested at 11 o'clock. I just want to make sure his eyes are all right. And I am pretty sure I need a little stronger glass. They slip fast when they slip. And I have so much to do with my eyes this year, I would rather do it in comfort. Tom seems the same kind of depressive as I am. This morning he was feeling particularly low. Also, he blames himself too much—too much. I wonder whether this is a family trait or whether he has learned it the hard way. Difficult to tell about such things—I guess I'd better get to my transition.

April 7 [6], Friday

Now the week is gone, the first week in April. I'll hate to see this month go because this is almost my favorite month of the year. I love it as much as I dislike March. This month growth begins to walk over the world. To me the word April has always seemed a beautiful word—a lilting word. May is soft but April still has a little sting, the fresh uncertainty and unpredictability of a very budding girl.

It is too bad that I write these long letters to you. I might be better employed in just sticking to my book. But I think I have explained my reason for it to you many times in an attempt to understand myself. Actually I do not think I lose much time with these letter pages. I think I would either be staring at a blank page or writing to someone else. I do know that I have always needed some kind of warm-up before going to work. And if I write to someone else I will be bored because I would have to tell things that happened last week or a month ago and I am not interested in those things. On the other hand, in this, there is rarely anything that did not happen mentally or physically within 24 hours. And in such things I still have an interest. So you see, I will continue with the letters. See how far I have got from the opening line—the week is gone. Can I be becoming one of those wandering bores? Perhaps so but the fact that it was so would not change it.

Let's see—I had Tom with me for two days. Had his eyes tested and they are all right except that he is wall-eyed and should make a strain to tighten the muscle of his eye, which wanders when he gets tired. I took him to school this morning and left him. I love him very dearly I guess because of his faults which are my faults. I know where his pains and his panics come from. He can be ruined or made strong in this exact little time. And now is the time when I must help him—not by bolstering him up but by forcing here and making him learn to balance there. Now I will try to get him at least one night every week.

Now comes the week end. You will be over for pages to type this afternoon. And I have no idea how many I have. It will be 62 handwritten, perhaps a hundred and thirty-five or forty typed. Maybe you will have some idea today. It is very hard to know. I have just changed the angle of my desk. All week I have been leaning over too far and my back is tired but such is the beauty of this wonderful drawing board that a change in angle and height completely changes my posture. I am going to do one thing though. I am going to paint it black. There is a glare on this light wood. I have a very soft black paint which should be very good. Anyway I will try it.

I am dawdling even more today because the window washer is here and there is a really slow man. But my time is up. I hope you have enjoyed Cathy so far. You are going to see more and more of her for a while. There's so much to write. Christ, this is going to be a long book. Such a long book. I think the window washer is nearly finished in my room so I will go back to my dear Cathy.

And there, Pat McPhat, is the week's work done. And I must say I am sorry. This has been a really challenging week and I must say I have enjoyed it. And I have finished just in time because Waverly has just come in with a chattering covey of girls and the house will not be very quiet anymore. I don't know how much I have done this week but I think it is a little over the quota I am trying to hold to. But I don't know. It is 14 pages for this week anyway. And it is enough. I am a little tired because the work has been really concentrated and packed, but it is always like that. It never changes. So what the hell. I'll paint my board and get to my bird cage. And I am a little pleased with myself this week because I have kept up my schedule in spite of many many interruptions. I'm glad about that.

I'll be seeing you soon.

April 8 [7], Saturday

You may as well declare page 63* a bust and forget it. I have managed to get it so dirty that I do not want to write on it. I really don't know how I got all the smudges on this poor paper —have been working in the garden, then painting and I guess this got in the way. No work today. I didn't intend to work anyway and this just confirms it. Yesterday was a good day. But it was a kind of a period. I could wish to get back to Adam and to take Cathy to him but this has to go its own way and take its own time. I can't seem to speed it. Sometimes I try to forget part but it goes in anyway whether I want it to or not. For instance— if I could in any way eliminate the next two scenes I would and

---

* In the notebook.

gladly. But I think they have to be there.* What they do is to build both Cathy's potential and to show that there is a point of weakness in her. It wouldn't be like other people's weakness but it will prove that everything does not go her way. Her effect on Edwards isn't abnormal I think. I have just invented a paperweight for an inclined desk that will drive you mad, it is so simple. You won't believe it when you see it. It is the kind of invention which for some reason makes people angry. I don't know why, but you know there are such things. I just showed it to Elaine and it made her mad so I guess it would get you too. I'll show it to you next Friday.

Now I am going to try to invent a hothouse. And suddenly I have an idea. This idea is for heating it. I wonder whether I could do that. How far would I have to tunnel for instance? It is certainly worth a try. Also I must find out about the oil heaters and electric heaters. Also must look for some glass. Secondhand glass. Elaine has just demanded a basket for incoming and out-, going mail. And I would be a silly thing if I could not make one. I guess I'll try. Once I had all such things but they go away somehow.

Monday, April 9

Another week, Pat, and I guess you will be glad. I get my new glasses this afternoon. And maybe that will be better. I will use them only on this floor and put the others on the other floors —one on third and one in kitchen, each on a hanger. Then no more running about. That will be good if I can remember. So many little things. I like the new black top to my desk. Makes it seem very nice indeed. And this week a change of posture which always makes a big difference. I must wash clothes this morning too. I take a certain satisfaction in washing my own T shirts, shorts and socks. Elaine would do it for me but I want to. My mother always taught me and apparently successfully that this was a part of privacy like washing your own teeth. Isn't it strange which things stick and which do not? You can't ever tell.

Now begins this other week of work and it is going to be a large one for me. You are always complaining about these pencil pages rubbing or running. I guess I'll have to spray them for you so you won't worry so much about them. I never saw anyone so

---

* End of Chapter 9.

miserish of copy as you are. Today I am going halfheartedly to boost my output—not violently but some. I feel I have slipped. Of course on a Monday I always feel that. But I'll see if I can't get in a few extra cracks this week.

You know how you have a feeling about a day? I feel that this is going to be an active one. I don't know why. The feeling is just there. Phones and things like that. No telling about such things and they don't often work out. Certainly they are not based on anything at all except that perhaps I want to be interrupted. It is amazing how much work rhythm you can lose by being off even for two days. I would like to work straight through to preserve the rhythm but I know that I would get too tired. I am well rested today but have lost my discipline. Don't know how one goes about preserving both freshness and discipline. Do you?

Had a good time at the South Pacific party Saturday night. At least five hundred people there. But in spite of the good time, a little sadness too because very deep in me I can never be a part of such things and I guess I have always wanted to. But something cuts me off always. I guess I am nearly at the age to be resigned about not being the things I guess as a child I wanted to be. The whole pattern Saturday night was oddly foreign to me. Maybe I too am a monster. I remember this sorrow at not being a part of things from very early in my childhood. Maybe from my very first birthday party.

And now my daily dawdling has reached its normal conclusion. And we go back to Cathy. I hope to get her to the point of meeting Adam either today or tomorrow. I have taken perhaps too long with her but I intend to take as much time as I need with everyone and everything. This is one book in which I intend to indulge every instinct I have. And believe me I shall. No reason why I should not. I do get a panic every once in a while about being interrupted. I feel that I will not be permitted to finish this book. But I must and will finish it. I have to. The Salinas papers have started to arrive. And they give me a sense of closeness with the region. And with that I guess it is time for me to go to work.

Now you see, Pat, what can happen to a man, to any man. And I hope you will take this as a lesson and a warning.

Now there, Pat, is a picture of pure violence. There is no way to avoid this. It was plotted from the first. And now we have come to the place where Adam meets his future wife. And it may be that this week I will get them ready for California. I may if I work hard even get them to the Salinas Valley, and I'll bet you will like that. You must be pretty tired of this long chapter. But I don't see how it could be otherwise than it was. I did three pages today. Maybe I will do the same tomorrow. I'll just have to see. That's all I can do. And so I leave this all for today.

April 10, Tuesday

Patrushka, if you only knew how bad we were last night you would be sad for us. You can't imagine such badness. We sat up all night long talking and drinking, just the two of us. It was five when we got to sleep. And of course I got up at 7:30. I feel fine but I could have done with a little more sleep. I have now made a new writing board to hold these pages. It is large and pretty. You would like it. I made it and painted it yesterday. Sometimes I think you will never understand me. My inventions you take lightly. My dream paperweight for an inclined desk you would laugh at. Well laugh, but we shall see who laughs last. When my paperweight covers the world. Then we shall see.

I am beginning to spray these pages with clear plastic. You have complained that they smudge. Well, they will never do it again—never. You can't even erase them when I get through. Try it and see from this page on.

Last night I read a few of the last pages to Elaine. She has not heard any for a long time. I told her that hereafter I would read to her on Thursday so she can keep up.

What shall I say now. A new day's work is starting and a new direction. It should be a chapter but I don't want a chapter. So it will be one of the large breaks.* Now I have finished with Catherine alone. Today she comes in contact with Adam and his brother. And their reaction to her is going to be a development of themselves. It is a day of dialogue, mostly dialogue. So far there has not been much except in bursts. And I had better get to it soon. I went for my glasses and they were not ready yesterday. I will have to go again today. Seems a shame. Well anyway I have an early start today in case anything should happen to interrupt me.

I must call Gwyn about the boys today. Must do that. Simply must. I have an idea besides.

---

* It became Chapter 10.

Got three dozen new pencils yesterday. I go through pencils fast and I love long ones—keep them very sharp and that is hard to do. Well, Pat, it is time for me to go to work. We shall see whether I can make these men begin to take shape. This is a hell of a story.

April 10, Tuesday, continued

Well I didn't get Cathy in because I wanted to paint the two men in their own words and also to give a kind of a look at their lives and the way people lived and talked then and the greyness of their lives. I had to do that because it has a definite bearing on what is going to happen. Such things have to be prepared for.

I hope you didn't feel that I was short this morning on the phone, about the criticism. Right now when I am only thinking ahead, it will do me no good. So write it all down and we'll go into it when the book is finished. As you remember I am pretty good about criticism. I want to warn you of only one thing. This is a different kind of a book and you must be sure that you do not dislike it for its difference. Also be very careful that you are sure that the thing you intend is not a carefully planted matter. I think that you must save any large criticism until the book is done or else you may find yourself trapped in this technique. You said this morning you had to sell x thousands of copies. I am sure, after all of our years together, you will not ask me to make one single change for the sake of sales except in terms of clarity. I am not writing for money any more now than I ever did. If money comes that is fine, but [if] I knew right now that this book would not sell a thousand copies, I would still write it. I want you to remember that, Pat. I have not changed in that respect even a little bit. Now my day's work is done and I am going to fix a chair and plant a plant. And good luck to all of us. And tomorrow Adam will find his future wife.

April 11, Wednesday

Today work is and is going to be slow. It is a slow day. All of my processes are slow. But no help for that. Oh! lord! I am coming to page 70 and in two or three weeks I shall pass 100 which will be I guess something like two hundred and fifty typed pages. That will be by the first of May at least. There is a very slow progression on this. I can't do it any other way. I feel calmer now that I have finished with the background of Cathy. It was a long haul. I don't know why I am slow today. But I am. Last night I had a session with Grieg,* my Norwegian publisher. He is a fine fellow and sells a lot of books. He just did a new edition of Mice and Men of 30,000. There are only 3,000,000 Norwegians. This edition would correspond to 1,500,000 copies in this country. He says in all editions he has sold over 70,000 copies of The Grapes of Wrath in Norway. This is really a fantastic figure.

My new glasses have come. I had them put in steel frames. Very light and I don't care what they look like because they are only for work. I can use my old glasses for casual things.

The human mind I believe is nothing but a muscle. Sometimes it has tone and sometimes not. And mine is not in very good tone right now. It is jumbled and slow and like a bad child. It refuses to obey me. I tell it to do something and it won't. In a short time now I will be angry with it and then it had better watch out. I am a hard master of the mind. I don't know. I don't know. Things operate so strangely. The fact of the matter is that I have several things on my mind at once and that poor instrument cannot take the overload.

Sometimes I wonder about things which are close to the unthinkable. And now I'll get to my knitting.

April 12, Thursday

I just begin to guess that this is a bad week. Energies ebb and flow and they have ebbed for me this week. Last night went to bed early but could not sleep for thinking of my story. It has been hard this week. I haven't fallen behind but I have picked up no lead either.

Tomorrow you will be coming around to pick up the week's work. And I don't feel very triumphant about it this week at all. There must be ups and downs, I guess. These are downs. I hate them. It is 10 o'clock. Elaine has gone to the country to see her friend and I miss her already. It will do her good to get out. She has been in the house all the time, painting mostly. So far the phone has not started to ring. I hope Louise does not come too late. It is almost doorbell and telephone time. I shall finish my day's

---

* Harald Grieg, head of Gyldendal, Oslo.

work and then go out on the street and walk. Then I go to see about Europe for next year—I'll talk to the people at Crowell since they want me to. But when I go I shall want to take my old post with the Herald Tribune. It does one thing—it lets me go just about where I want to. And besides I like working for them. I think I can do more relaxed work than ever. Alexander of Crowell Publishing says that John Hersey and I are the only two good reporters in the world now. Flattering but not true. I have not much time nor space for comment this morning. And because of the slump I feel reluctant to work but I have to. You know I have lost practically no work time since I started this book. That is pretty good I think—don't you. There goes the doorbell. It is starting and so must I. So to work.

Now I move the page. The work is coming a little easier or maybe I am just getting used to it. And I am getting closer to California. Next week I'll be there. And I don't want to speed it up. I want to go into this feeling of Adam's and also I want to give very good reasons for the move. It should not be so very hard. I have to go to Cathy now. And I am really dawdling today more than I should maybe. Well let's see what I can do with Cathy.

April 13 [FRIDAY]

Well, big news—Zapata will be made. Colliers or rather Crowell do want me to make the big trip next January. And I will surely have this book done by then. My workbench will be cut today and will get here either today or tomorrow. All very exciting. You will be coming over for copy this afternoon. It is such a big day. I think I know how the day's work will go. And I am going to get to work on it early. It is a beautiful spring day. I would like to be out in it but can't. That is just one of the penalties. I'll bet the chore of typing from this is getting bad. But it has to be done. There's no getting away from that. Elaine is painting the maid's room today. We work very hard for our servants. Everyone does. But Louise is good and faithful. It would never occur to her to paint her room. That's why she is a servant. It has advantages and disadvantages. And now to work.

I must admit that this is a very messy page but I can't help that. It's just that way. Next week I will try to make it more neat.

Another week, Pat. I think and I hope my slump is over but it is very hard to know. I was thinking after you came over on Friday—I hope you haven't too clear an idea of how this book is going to be, because if it doesn't turn out that way, you are going to be disappointed and I should hate that. You might get preconceptions and you must not do that. This is a grey day but of the kind I like. Reminds me of mornings in Salinas when I hated to get up and go to school. And I hated to get up this morning too.

Now my mental disciplines are a little relaxed by the week end. And you know of course that many times before I finish this book I shall hate it with a deadly hatred. I shall detest the day when I started it. It will seem the poorest piece of crap that was ever set down. This feeling will reach a fine peak on about the 500th page. Once I pass that I will continue to work in a state of shock. And when it is done I will be lost for a long time.

I want to ask and even beg one thing of you—that we do not discuss the book any more when you come over. No matter how delicately we go about it, it confuses me and throws me off the story. So from now on let's do the weather or fleas or something else but let's leave the book alone. In that way we'll have some surprises. I know you won't mind this once you see why. Once it is done, you may tear it to shreds if you wish and I won't object, and I'll go along with you, but right now both you and I forget the delicate sets of balances involved. There are no good collaborations and all this discussion amounts to collaboration. So, we'll do that, if you don't mind. And let's stop counting pages, too. I am not being difficult I hope. It is just too hard on me to try to write, defend and criticise all at the same time. I can quite easily do each one separately. Let me keep the literary discussions on these poor pages. Then we will have no quarrels. I know you make fun of my inventions and my designs. But they are the same thing as writing. I come from a long line of inventors. This is in my blood. We are improvisors and will continue to be. Now I find there is a great suspicion and fear of inventors and the first attack is always based on the fact that they are crazy—and maybe they are. My father was not an inventive man and he always said the Hamiltons were crazy. It was because he did not understand them. One is always crazy. Also the inventions of the Hamiltons did not make money. Money always removes the charge of craziness.

Now I can get back to the book. Today or tomorrow this chapter* ends. It has a lot of facets left but they are small ones. It will have become one of the world's longest chapters. You will wonder why Cathy married Adam. Don't worry—she will tell you but not yet. She will tell you when she tells him and you will just have to wait three long chapters for that. And I guess now is the time— Today Adam-Charles, Adam-Cathy, Cathy-Charles, Adam-Charles. And it will end on that. Maybe I can finish it today but I don't think so. And thus we leave you for today.

April 17, Tuesday

I guess my note of yesterday was pretty silly. When one lives completely in a book as I do in this one the determination not to talk about it is a really futile thing. So there's another thing to disregard. These notes are loaded with futilities. However, that's the way it is. Now that chapter is done and you'll have to admit it was abrupt. I go now to another Hamilton chapter which will also be a transition chapter. But before I go into that, I must say I am pleased about Pascal's † lecture. And I hope you will tell him I am. He is making great progress all along the line and probably in some fields we know nothing about, which is as it should be. I am amused at your reaction to my charge of your commercialism. All right I apologize. You rose to the bait beautifully though. That is another of my inventions. And I have a couple more which I am holding back. Sometimes I wish I could throw everything into this work. If my total energy went into it, I could finish it in two months. But I would not have the fun that I am having now. And I can tell you quite truthfully that I have never had such a good time with a book. Maybe this doesn't make it good but it surely makes it a pleasure to me. And don't think it is always easy.

Now—let's see—today I want to try to get circus tickets for Saturday for my boys. And they are very hard to get. But I'm going to try. Still my workbench has not come. Don't know why not. It should have been here Saturday. I can't get my room in order until it comes. You know I just had a really brilliant idea about the workbench. What a good idea. And I will surely put it into use too.

---

* End of Chapter 11 and end of Part One.
† Pascal Covici, Jr., in his junior year at Harvard, gave an informal lecture on Steinbeck's work for an evening course, primarily for high-school teachers.

I suppose my mind seems flighty today. Maybe it is but actually today must start with lyricism. And do you know I have no idea what chapter it is. I think it is #4 but am not sure.* I will call it that anyway. I have thought a great deal about the one sentence heading for the large paragraphs. It might be a very good thing to do.

Now I have left the east coast and I will never go back to it. You may think I stayed in Connecticut too long but I really had to give the background of the Trasks. It would be meaningless if you didn't know what they came from and what sent them to California. But now they are there. And I shall get them there with a sentence. The year is 1892. The reason for that is that I want the son of Cathy to be 60 years old in 1952 when the book comes out, because I want the grandson of Cathy to be 20 years old in 1952. These ages are important to the book. The one person you are not going to understand in this book is Cathy and that is because you don't know her. Cathy sometimes tells the truth but she is like my friend [. . .] You can believe her lies but when she tells the truth it is not credible. And I guess now it is time to get to work and stop the nonsense.

Now, Pat, I know it is unorthodox to put in the preceding article of faith but if you will remember back, I said the teller would be opinionated. I have not taken it clear away from the story and I want to say it. And as for my comments on the story, I find it or rather I feel that it is more direct and honest to set it down straight than to sneak it in so that the reader will not know or suspect it as opinion. As you will have discovered even in the amount I have written, the technique of this book is an apparent lack of technique and I assure you that is not easy. The Trask story was a rather dreadful one. I think it is good to settle back and regard it quietly—to give the reader a rest and to let him think about it and perhaps to direct a little what he thinks about it. Anyway, that is what I am going to do. Reflection is no bad thing although I must say in this time it is not a popular pastime. I feel good about the Trask section and I must say I am glad it is done. I am glad they are in California. But I'll tell you what I am going to do. I'm going to bring them to California and then go to the Hamiltons. And with this chapter I think you will finally become aware of the counterpoint. So I will go on with my day's work and good luck to me.

---

* It became Chapter 13.

April 18, Wednesday

Last night I stayed up too late talking to Odets and Juan Negrin.* So I am tired today and was reluctant to get up. This will pass in a short while and I will go on working. I am content with the transition in Chapter 4, aren't you? Read it to Elaine last night and she liked it. Today is a very busy day. Kazan is coming over in the afternoon to discuss summer plans. I am going to try to get circus tickets for Saturday. Very hard to get. Still building my carpenter's bench but I will be doing that for a long time. I may have to get a sheet of Masonite for it to cover it. So many things to do. I wonder if I will ever get them done. Well I just have to, just have to. If I can get circus tickets for Saturday or Sunday, will get the boys the day before and keep them overnight.

Well today MacArthur † parade. I will keep off the street. This is a frightful political build-up and only now does its purpose begin to be apparent. It is sad to see the awful machinations of the little-souled men. How cynical they must be. I suppose that if I had any sense at all, I would not write today but I am going to anyway. It would be a great joke on the people in my book if I just left them high and dry, waiting for me. If they bully me and do what they choose I have them over a barrel. They can't move until I pick up a pencil. They are frozen, turned to ice standing one foot up and with the same smile they had yesterday when I stopped. I have one bad little episode to put in before I go on to a new saga of the Hamiltons. It's hard to know which story to tell first—there are so many. But I have to get to them to make a counterpoint for the bleak opening of the Trasks. And now I guess I must get to it.

Now, there's the first episode. And now we'll do a little jumping about. And maybe you think it is about time. I have stayed very close to this one story although I must say it covered a lot of ground. My wish is that when my reader has finished with this book, he will have a sense of belonging in it. He will actually be a native of that Valley. He needn't know intimately a great many people but he will have a nodding acquaintance with

---

* Clifford Odets, the dramatist; Juan Negrin, neurosurgeon in New York and friend of Steinbeck, who referred Covici to him (see pages 110 and 126).

† General of the Army Douglas MacArthur.

very many. I want it to be a life experience. I would like the reader to forget where he read the little essays and even think he invented them himself. That's not too much to ask, is it? Now, in spite of the questions I won't let you ask yet, I think you do think the book is going pretty well. I think it is myself. It is getting a heavy tread from the weight of incidents. Its constantly changing style is beginning to take effect. I hope by these changes of mood and approach to remove tiresomeness in a long novel. And there is another thing I have never discussed with you. If a man has a too pat style, his reader can after a little time keep ahead of him. I mean the reader will know what is coming by how it is done. And I am trying to remove this possibility by constant change. And now back to work for the second half of my day's work.

April 19, Thursday

Now comes another day but this day I am not tired. The good sleep sharpened me and I feel refreshed. Today is Mac-Arthur day and that big hunk of sacrosanct shit will be making the air horrid with his platitudes. I get such a sense of dishonesty from this man. Wonder what his wife thinks of him.

I should not take much time for comment today because I am anxious to get into the change. Today I introduce the Hamiltons to Adam Trask and my purpose, as you will understand, will be to put down the Salinas Valley from a county man's viewpoint. To show the fine hopes of the people and their ingeniousness. To develop the kind of mind Samuel had and to indoctrinate Adam with the flavor of the Valley. Don't forget he is now a Valley man. And that may be enough subject for one day. Elaine is always amazed that I cover so much territory in one day's work. And what I have just said will be quite enough for one day's work. So. I think I will get to it. Maybe there will be other notes later—I might tell you that I invented a tool rack this day which is going to be the glory of the world. You will marvel when you see it, and with good reason for there has never been a tool rack like this one. And I will build it all today. You will be able to see it tomorrow.

And now has come the time for work to start and I am very early too. I will be through with writing at a reasonable hour. And now to go.

There's the halfway mark. I wanted to put that in to show how the people felt about the country and about the Hamiltons. I think that is necessary. Relationships in a country are the most revealing part of it. If I can get those down I'll be pleased if I can do it well and now I'll go on.

April 20, Friday

The last writing day of the week. I feel rather tired and I hope I get through today but it is one of those which seem insuperable. For one thing I'm fighting off a cold and that is one thing I just don't want and can't use now. And with it has come a kind of dullness. I can hope for one thing today. A book sometimes moves on by inertia and I do hope this one has now enough momentum to struggle on. Boys this afternoon and circus tomorrow and I must be well for that. I think after a while the circus bores them but it has great eminence—the going to it. And I must say I like it too.

My brain is not a very good instrument today—not very good at all. And it is an important day in the book. I wanted to go into the nature of the Valley. And I will but I wanted it to be clear and sharp and effective. I am trying desperately to remember the sound of my grandfather's speech. And maybe my memory is not entirely accurate but at least I am trying to give a feeling of it. He made a nice use of figures. And I am trying to approximate them. Being a well borer he knew the earth very well, and being an inventor he was always trying to improve on it. But it is going to be hard going today. Thank goodness I have an early start. MacArthur will be panjoraming about today and it will be noisy. Our good shy proconsul (the ham) is having a field day. I'll have to set my book against the yammer. These same crowds who shriek for him today will turn on him tomorrow. Well I don't think he will be president. Two speeches like that of yesterday would do for him. He mispronounces words with a godly authority. I detest him. He has absolutely no humility. But back to my first premise. I don't feel any better. But I have to. You'll be over for copy this afternoon. And dam it, I'm tired. Going to get coffee and then go to work now.

Later. I'm coming out of it. The story of the sofa is true. The Williams girls—one of them just died at 85—remembered it all their lives. In fact all of the Hamilton stories are true.

April 20, continued

Well that section and my week's work are done. It went longer than a day's work but I wanted to finish it up. And it is my hope that I gave some picture of Samuel Hamilton. Garrulous he is but he has flair. And that is good. I wonder if I got the aliveness of his brain, his mechanical ability and the curious poetry he put about him. I can remember the lilt in his speech and he must surely have used fine figures of speech because I see him surrounded with all manner of birds and beasts and qualities of light. And I wanted to set down what the soil was like. This builds so slowly but I hope it builds. I think next I will go to my mother and do a sketch of her life ending with her airplane ride which I think is very funny. I see no reason for not skipping about in time with the Hamiltons. There are so many of them that if I tried to keep them all going at the same time it would be confusing. Therefore I think the Hamilton chapters will be sketches of the children's lives. The next Trask chapter is going to be a long one, very long. It goes through the settling of the ranch, the birth of the twins, the first two years of their lives and Cathy's departure. This is an extremely long chapter and one which will take at least two weeks to write. Then will come the life in Salinas of Cathy, I think. And now that is enough for now. I'm going to do some other kind of work for a while and try to settle down. I'm jumpy with fatigue today.

April 22, Sunday

No work today but perhaps a few notes. Circus yesterday with the boys and a good fine time. They wanted cow-horn horns and rubber tulips and got them. Then went to dinner. Lost a big filling from a tooth which angered me but I would rather go to the dentist now than this summer. Today I painted my workbench. It is now finished and I am glad. I shall begin to do my little doodly work on it.

Tomorrow to work again and even though I was tired on Friday I shall be glad to get back to it. I'm going to do my mother's story tomorrow, actually a little biography of anecdotes.

April 23, Monday

Dear Pat—another week. I must say that even with the boys and the circus I did not get far from the book. I have thought of little else. It's a strange thing how one can become so obsessed that there is always the double thing—the book and whatever else is going on and both running parallel. I guess it has to be that way.

They say, and I expect truly, that if a man could see his whole life, he would never live it. He would kill himself instantly. Something like this happens on the week-end days when I do not work. I lift my eyes out of the details of the little day's work and a panic crashes on me. The size and the difficulty rise up and smack me. And yet it is necessary to look at the whole thing now and then. It's like swimming with your head down or up. It cuts your speed to raise your head but at least you know where you are going. And it occurs to me that this may be a very good book —but with a slight variation it may be gibberish. Since you told me what the girl said about wanting to get on with the story and not stop for comment, I have thought a good deal about that. It is going to be one of the most constant criticisms of this book. People are insistent to get on with their lives too and not to think about them. It will also be said that I could well leave the Hamiltons out of the book because they do not contribute directly nor often to the Trask development. And I must be very willful about this, because this is not a story about the Trasks but about the whole Valley which I am using as a microcosm of the whole nation. It is not a romanza. I know I will have that war to fight.

I was pleased about Pascal's lecture about my work and I wish I could have heard it. I might have learned something valuable to me. For we work in our own darkness a great deal with little real knowledge of what we are doing. I think I know better what I am doing than most writers but it still isn't much. I don't know why I am thinking now of criticism since I will not let it change one single thing about the story or the method. It is almost the autobiography of the Valley. I think I had better put down a section on the place names of the Valley because sometimes they seem contrived unless it is known that there are many strange and interesting names in the region. Don't you think perhaps this might be a good time to do this. People are interested in names. At least I think they are. I'll put it in anyway.

It is now getting on to time to go to work. On the last page Adam bought the Bordoni place. Now I am going to stay away from Adam and Cathy for a while to give Cathy a chance to get along with her pregnancy. Then when you start with them again you will have a sense of time lapse. So I am going off into several other things—first the place names, then some of the stories of my mother. I'll stick with her until I am ready to go back to the Trasks again. So I will with the other children of Samuel. And now it is time to go to work.

April 24, Tuesday

Day by day it goes. And little by little I am trying to build up the picture. It may seem to take too great a time but I have a theory (good god, the number of theories you are subjected to). There are some people who deeply and basically dislike theories and are hostile to speculations. These are usually unsure people who, whirling in uncertainties, try to steady themselves by grabbing and tightly holding on to facts. And it is getting to be even sadder because facts have a way of changing nowadays, at least of changing their implications. This leaves the fact person on a limb. Speculation or theory-making on the other hand is simply a little game of pattern-making of the mind. The theory hater cannot believe that it is important. To such a person a theory is a lie until it is proven and then it becomes a truth or a fact. But there's no joy in it. Now—to get to my theory. You have said and Harold* has said often that a big book is more important and has more authority than a short book. There are exceptions of course but it is very nearly always true. I have tried to find a reasonable explanation for this and at last have come up with my theory, to wit: The human mind, particularly in the present, is troubled and fogged and bee-stung with a thousand little details from taxes to war worry to the price of meat. All these usually get together and result in a man's fighting with his wife because that is the easiest channel of relief for inner unrest. Now—we must think of a book as a wedge driven into a man's personal life. A short book would be in and out quickly. And it is possible for such a wedge to open the mind and do its work before it is withdrawn leaving quivering nerves and cut tissue. A long book, on the other hand, drives in very slowly and if only in point of time remains for a while. Instead of cutting and leaving, it allows the mind to rearrange itself to fit around the wedge. Let's carry the analogy a little farther. When the quick wedge is withdrawn, the tendency of the mind is quickly to heal itself exactly as it was before the attack. With the long book perhaps the healing has been warped around the shape of the wedge so that when the

---

* Harold K. Guinzburg, president of The Viking Press.

wedge is finally withdrawn and the book set down, the mind cannot ever be quite what it was before. This is my theory and it may explain the greater importance of a long book. Living with it longer has given it greater force. If this is true a long book, even not so good, is more effective than an excellent short book. How do you like that theory?

Now to get back to my book in particular. I feel that it is important to go into the school system at some length just as I think it will be necessary to go into the whorehouse situation also. These were two facets of the culture of the period and both were important. In fact, when you come right down to it, everything was important.

I am learning many things—some of them not very flattering to me, but all of them important. I am learning how specialized I am and also that the degree of specialization is also the degree of limitations. Let me give you an example of what I mean. When I work on a book to this extent and with this concentration, it means that I am living another life. As it goes along, increasingly I give to the second life more than to the first. Then I must be very hard to live with in real life, not because I am mean but because I am vague. Things ordinarily done are forgotten. My expression must be one of fogged stupidity—my responses slow. It is during this time that a woman gets first restless, then uneasy, then angry. I don't know what to do about it but there it is. And a book like this goes on for such a long time. You can read it in a few days but it takes years to think and write. It must be a great chore to live with if you are not writing it. This time I am making a distinct and constant effort to keep both lives going but even then I forget. But anyway I am trying. There is one other thing—the function which at a distance seems romantic and colorful must on daily contact become dull and usual and machine-like. It is bound to. And finally it may become a rival, an enemy. This is not inevitable but it has happened to me twice. End note for now.

I got a little ahead of myself today. I like to hold the word rate down because if I don't, it will get hurried and I will get too tired one day and not work the next. The slow, controlled method is best. But I got into my mother's airplane ride and it got out of hand. But I used self-control and did not let her actually get into the airplane. That will come tomorrow. And I think I will finish the section of her life tomorrow. It is a strange feeling to be taking people who are close to me apart and putting them on paper. But I see no reason why I should not. They are mine and I can do what I like with them.

It has been a good day of work with no harm in it. I have sat long over the desk and the pencil has felt good in my hand. Outside the sun is very bright and warm and the buds are swelling to a popping size. I guess it is a good thing I became a writer. Perhaps I am too lazy for anything else.

Now I will leave you until tomorrow. I have letters to write. Sometimes the old terror comes up in the night but thank goodness it is pretty much gone in the daytime, except right at first and not every day even then. Now I must stop this dawdling and get to my other work in my other life.

April 25, Wednesday

The week and the month going fast. And I shall cross the hundredth handwritten page before the first of May. I figure it will take about four hundred to finish the book, so by the first of May I will be one quarter of the way through and that is right on schedule. If it continues this way I will finish just about when I thought I would. I started active work on Feb. 19 so it is just a little over two months. At that rate the book should only take 8 months and should be done by the first of November, but that is allowing for no accidents whatever and it would be an odd year when something drastic did not happen. I am allowing two months for accidents and will figure to be done by Christmas. But I am not going to speed up. I just can't do it and keep with it for that length of time. Two of these pages is just about right for the pace of this book. And it is odd how every book has its own pace. The Grapes of Wrath was headlong and I don't want this one to be. Slow and easy does it. I must say that I think of very little else now. I repainted my table and it is not quite dry so I am writing on a cardboard cover today.

You made a bad mistake when you suggested that you buy a tool for my desk. There is only one that I want and it is expensive. I have everything else. But I do not have very small tools for very tiny work. Such I could use and would even make you something.

Good early start today. A grey day but I like it. Almost like a Monterey day. Thinking last night about how many lives I have led and how much time I've wasted. Not a good way to think but sometimes you can't control it. Little evil things rise up like gas bubbles out of a swamp. And maybe it is a good thing for it to come out now and then. Who knows what poisons in the mind can do. But what silliness to mourn over lost time. I have a feeling impossible of verification that worry is a pathological function of some time required by the human soul for its well-being in greater or less degree. I think that worry is a constant and that only after it rises to the conscious mind do we find a direction for it to take. If this were not so, we would not worry about such ridiculous things. But, given the feeling, we always find something on which to use it. (Theory?) I will constipate you with theories and drug you with speculations. That's funny, isn't it?

Now we will go back to the book. I think and hope I am going to finish the chapter today. And that will be all about my mother. I feel that she is not as well drawn as some of the others and I also feel that this is natural. We cannot know objectively about one who is so close. I don't see how we can anyway. The great story of the Hamiltons is that of Uncle Tom and his sister Dessie and of the death of Dessie and Tom's suicide. I am going to do that one fairly late in the book because there is no Hamilton story to top it—a dreadful and beautiful story. And now to my day's work.

Well that's done and I hope you will like it. And now I am ready to go back to the Trasks again. And this will be another very long chapter taking in the birth of the twins, their meaning and the departure of Cathy. This is a very long and extremely important chapter.* It will be highly detailed. And you must not worry about losing Cathy. She will be always present even if she only comes into the story a few more times. In this chapter the relations between the Trasks and the Hamiltons become open and now I suppose the introduction is over and we are ready to move down the century. If it has seemed to take a long time, it had to be that way. Kazan is coming in Thursday about two o'clock to work. I think I will get up about four or five in the morning so that I will surely get my day's work done before he arrives. I'm getting a fixation about not missing days even though I know I will miss many before this book is done. I just must expect that. But every day I don't miss is a help and a treasure.

---

* It became Chapters 15 and 16.

The light shines on me sometimes and the sadness of remembering [grows full?] sometimes but there is no help for these extremes and they must be done.

And now I must leave you until tomorrow.

April 26, Thursday

I think I am crazy to try to work today. Every bone in my body aches and I have no idea why. Maybe a little twitch of flu. I have been very lucky about that. Even my right hand and arm aches. Maybe it will be better later. And my spirit is very low. Well it is still early. I may be better later. I'm afraid I'm going to lose tomorrow. Kazan wants me to do a final bit on the script and he says he can't work in the afternoon. Well, it will be the first day I guess in a long time so I should not mourn. And I have all day today. Might even go a little over. I am certainly not fit now. Lord! I hope I pick up later. I collapsed discreetly. Elaine has her problems today and I don't want to be one of them. And my recovery is very rapid. I am feeling better. I thought I could bull it through and I was wrong. Sometimes it is a very great virtue. I get very boastful about what I can do. It is no bad thing to be brought down to size.

The day is going and I am trying to get up the initial strength to get into my book. There's a basic shove and I don't seem quite capable of it. Strange, isn't it? But at least I am getting dogged about it and I may just sit here until I dam well make it even if the warm-up is not taking effect very quickly. Yes, sir, it is really putting up a fight today. I don't feel well but it is more than that. Maybe the basic laziness creeping back—who knows. And surely it is not lack of material. I am brimming with material. I've *got* to get to it. I simply must. I guess it will be about time now to force it through.

Well, there it goes for better or for worse. And there is no harm done I guess. All the little things break in sometimes. I guess it is true that big and strong things are much less dangerous than small soft weak things. Nature (whatever that is) makes the small and weak reproduce faster. And that is not true of course. The ones that did not reproduce faster than they died, disappeared. But how about little faults, little pains, little worries. The cosmic ulcer comes not from great concerns, but from little irritations. And great things can kill a man but if they do not he is stronger and better for them. A man is destroyed by the duck nibblings of nagging, small bills, telephones (wrong number), athlete's foot, ragweed, the common cold, boredom. All of these are the negatives, the tiny frustrations, and no one is stronger for them.

Today in my bumbling, I have made two shelves and bored many holes and started on your box. It will take time but it is started. You said you wanted a box to put things in but you didn't say what things so I will have to judge what things you would put in a box without falling in yourself. And now, it is time to ring off.

It is just no good and I am going to throw it away. I haven't had many bust days but this has been calamitous from the start. Also I am not going to worry Elaine about it. She has a million things to do. And I'm not going to worry myself about it either. It is just a loss. Maybe I can pick it up next week. That means two days will be lost this week. It may take me quite a bit to pick it up but maybe the rest will do me good. I'm going to try it anyway. I'm not going to worry about it but I wish I could know what caused it. Went to bed early last night, read happily, slept happily. Got up early and suddenly felt terrible—just terrible. Fought that off and was drained dry. Then I forced the work and it was as false and labored and foolish as anything I have ever seen. I tried to kid myself that it only seemed bad but it really *was* bad. So out it goes. And what do you suppose could have caused it? I just don't know. There seem to be dead places in a man or like lit

April 30, Monday

Well, I pulled a complete bust on Thursday, and Friday Kazan came to work. So I lost two days last week. This is why I give myself the leeway of time. I do not know what happened Thursday. I just went completely to pieces. I suppose it can and does happen to everyone. Last night we went to two parties—one at Faye Emerson's and the other at the Stork Club for Joan Crawford. But it was all right. I didn't drink anything and we were home by 11 o'clock. Not much sleep but that doesn't matter. I got plenty of rest.

Maybe it was the new section that frightened me off. Like starting a new book or a sequel to an old one. I think I'll get it going today. Must do it. Among the other misfortunes last week two inlays fell out, and until I can get them replaced there is a constant minor-key headache and toothache but not bad enough to stop work. Did I tell you that I went down to look at a piano—beautiful instrument—and bought it. It won't be ready for a month but when it is, Pascal can play for us if he will. And the piano is far my favorite instrument in the world. So maybe he will.

Tom's winning the prize* was a fine thing. He pretended he didn't care about it but when they called out his name he cried "Here I am!"

Now the day progresses and I haven't put down a word yet but it is coming and I am almost ready. Almost! I have the tone now. And an amazing number of pretty girls are passing by my window. I like pretty girls very much but I am old enough now so that I don't have to associate with them. And that's a relief.

Of course—that's the way it has to go. So simple when it finally comes to you. That's the way it is. You fight a story week after week and day by day and then it arranges itself in your hands. I'm going to allow myself 20 more minutes before I lash into it. I'm trying to figure how to finish your box and I think finally I know. I just figured it out. And it should be very pretty. And I know how I am going to line it too. That was giving me trouble. There was no reason for it but I am naïve and I never learn—I guess I never will. In a way I am glad for it keeps me learning all the time—even if it is the same thing over and over. Now I have taken the black off my desk again, clear down to the wood, and have put a green blotter down. I am never satisfied with my writing surface.

And now my lazy time is over—really over I think—and my allotted time for dawdling is over too.

There—that's done and I think the rhythm re-established. Anyway the bloc is broken.

May 1, Tuesday

Up very early today. I want to get into it and also I want to get finished. I have many projects. Many. And tonight guests. Frank and Lynn Loesser and Fred and Portland Allen. Frank goes away tomorrow. That is why it has to be tonight. I'm going to call you pretty soon about a project that should appeal to you. Got to thinking so hard last night that I could not stop. New rela-

---

* For designing a Safety First poster.

tionship but a supplementary one. I want to go a little into Cathy today and also into Lee the Chinese. I have known so many of them. Remarkable people the California Chinese. Also I want to bring Samuel into the picture and relate him to the house. This I can do I think. I will work very hard today. The images are back disturbing the clear water of my thinking and it seems good to me. There won't be a great deal of dawdling today. I may even go over my quota so that I can go and look at dining-room tables tomorrow. We are eating on a serving table that bumps my knees pretty badly. And we stick up card tables too. I'm just about to start now. Maybe I should phone and ask your advice about the Ritz stuff.* You can always find out things. And I'll bet you will for me too. Now you are going to like Lee. He is a philosopher. And also he is a kind and thoughtful man. And beyond all this he is going to go in the book because I need him. The book needs his eye and his criticism which is more detached than mine. I have a fine early start today so I shall get to it soon. Starts with Cathy, goes to Lee, brings in Samuel. And then Samuel's relationship with Lee, and Lee's relationship to Adam and to Cathy. Lee's attitudes will if anything be clearer than mine. Also Lee has to raise the boys. And now I am ready to go to work.

May 2, Wednesday

Well today I will get rid of Samuel's ride to the Trask place. Since Lee is going to be with the book for quite a long time, I thought it was a good time to get to know him. I am at work very early so I can go down and look at dining-room tables today. And then to the dentist. I like to go to the dentist after work. The usual dull ache that follows is hard to work through.

I wonder what you found out about the things from the Ritz Carlton. Maybe you will phone me about it today. Also I want to phone John O'Hara about the tip of Long Island. We might want to go there for the summer. It is a warm day—very summery. Time to open the windows.

I should reach page 100 this week and that will be about between one quarter and one third of the book. I just worked it out. It is running about 800 words to the page or a little over. So

---

* Furnishings from the old Ritz Carlton Hotel in New York were being offered for sale before its demolition. The Steinbecks were looking for doors.

it will not be far from 80,000 words this week. And now I must get to it.

May 3, Thursday

Fine rest last night and I feel wonderful. We are going to join that library you mentioned.* Yesterday on my walk home I went to look at a beautiful car, a Jaguar Speedster, one of the handsomest cars in the world. I may get one for the European trip. † It has no luggage space but perhaps a trunk can be devised or is made. If I could have one delivered in Rome, it would be fine. Then either sell it or bring it home. I must start getting passports next week. I like to do things in advance. I already have a man looking into routes, etc. And I just had a brilliant idea about the car—how it could be done, I mean. I will investigate. I am so full of plans today but I guess I always am. This is no change. I just had a fine idea. And maybe all of this may seem to you to be thinking away from the book—but it is not, because the book never leaves me now. Oh! Lord, I feel good! It scares me a little. As though it could not last. Well, it does last a little. Do you remember the critic, I think it was Sterling North, who gave me hell in a review because I was working in an air-conditioned office? I'll bet he would hate me for feeling good too. He would think I am not suffering enough. And maybe I am not.

I have brought the nightingale up to my workroom to be with me while I work. This bird was wilting away for lack of company. He pretends to be frightened but he loves company. And now to the book. Today I am going into plans for the Salinas Valley. I am going to set down Adam's plans for his life. The fact that he isn't going to get even one of them has no emphasis whatever. Plans are real things and not experience. A rich life is rich in plans. If they don't come off, they are still a little bit realized. If they do, they may be disappointing. That's why a trip described becomes better the greater the time between the trip and the telling. I believe too that if you can know a man's plans, you know more about him than you can in any other way. Plans are daydreaming and this is an absolute measure of a man.

---

* Probably the New York Society Library, a private subscription library at 53 East 79th Street. He did not join.
† Steinbeck did not buy a Jaguar at this time, but bought one in Europe in 1954.

Thus if I dwell heavily on plans, it is because I am trying to put down the whole man. What a strange life it is. Inspecting it for the purpose of setting it down on paper only illuminates its strangeness. There are strange things in people. I guess one of the things that sets us apart from other animals is our dreams and our plans. Now that is enough of that.

The day is lovely and sunny. And I am sunny but not lovely. Time is creeping upon me while I sit and put down my wayward words. I suppose by this means I put off the discipline of the book but I can do that no longer. So here I go.

May 4, Friday

The week is ending now and it has been such a full one. Many things have happened and had to be taken care of. I do believe that it will grow worse for a time now. There are lots of details having nothing to do with work that must be solved every day. And with my single-track mind that is difficult. But I believe I can do it. If a little raddled tone creeps in, that will be the reason for it. Going to the country tomorrow to look for a summer place up around Quogue. I have never been there. You will come over today and I will have two weeks lacking two days of work for you. I think it is fitting to come to page 100 on the week end, don't you. I wish I could have kept up my record of never missing a day but maybe that was a ridiculous hope.

I do not want to dawdle today because I have so many things to do. Got to my desk before 8 o'clock which is good for me. And I'll work as hard as I can at it. The flower carts are going by in the street today and they are very beautiful. Every week they get more colorful. Really beautiful.

Now it is time for me to try to get to work. Maybe I can add another note to this week afterwards but somehow I doubt it.

May 7, Monday

And now, dear Pat, we come to the second hundred mss. pages. It is a kind of minor milestone but not very important. The third hundred pages will be very important. Then I will have to be bending in toward my finish.

First let me say that we went the length of Long Island Saturday, slept twelve hours at Montauk and drove back yesterday and slept very long. I feel completely rested. We saw enough of Long Island to know we do not want to spend the summer there. It is just wrong. Some time this week we may go up to the Cape to look there. In our quest we have discovered that some people dislike every place we start for—but dislike with intensity. It is possible that we will fly up to Martha's Vineyard this week end and if we do, I will work next week end so there will be no loss of time in work. I'll just have to do it that way. I am well and healthy I guess and prepared to start the new 80,000. And the story holds my interest as I hope it holds yours. It is a strange thing, a story. It changes so much all the time. And there is no way to stop that.

I was so glad that Dorothy came over the other afternoon. We have been lax about inviting her but that has been so with everyone. From week to week we thought the furniture for our library would be here. We wanted the room furnished before we invited people and now we know that it won't be ready before the end of the summer or the fall so we have had the spring of waiting for nothing.

It is a lovely day. If New York could stay this way no one would ever leave it.

I guess I should start work on your present. It is going to take a very long time to do. And I hope it is going to be beautiful and that you will like it. Surely it will be made with care but it is in a material new to me so I will have to learn as I go. And that is difficult and may have a number of failures as you very well know. However, I am going to try it. Never let it be said that I was afraid to try something just because I didn't know anything about it. By trial and error I will finish it, believe me I will. And it will be unique also. I can promise you that.

Now to the book. This is a brooding time in the book—a time of waiting and a time in which dangers poke up their heads. Why doesn't Adam listen when Cathy says she will be going away? I don't know. Men don't listen to what they don't want to hear. I know I didn't and every man I think is somewhat the same—every man. I must point that out very clearly. Adam has a picture of his life and he will continue to maintain his picture against every influence until his world comes down. I know that this is true. But I must make it convincing. And I guess now the time has come to put my thesis into action. I hope I have a good week. I really hope so. You can breathe a little prayer for it if you wish. Also, this week I must go back on a rigid diet to break the plateau I am on. I really want to lose 10–15 more pounds. Then I will be about right I think. Discipline—discipline!

May 7, *continued*

Now, Pat, when you have read 101–102 you should have some quality of my grandfather's mind, put in on purpose. As you said the other day—he would know. But what you didn't say is that he would doubt his knowledge. I think most people doubt their instinctive knowledge. And I hope you will find this home ride effective. I meant it to be a matter largely of mood. And perhaps it is. I hope so. And that will be just about all for today.

May 8, *Tuesday*

I think yesterday's work had a kind of energy in the design. I went to the dentist afterwards. Now I only need a cleaning. Waverly is sick this morning. She has a bug that has hung on for a long time. Today is going to be slower but who cares. I have all day to do it. This is the kind of a day I like. I can do a few sentences, then stop and enjoy them. Most days there is something else that has to be done afterwards, but this Tuesday, if I don't finish until evening, it doesn't make a bit of difference. And how nice that is.

I am singularly without nerves today. Marshall seems to have answered MacArthur at every point but without rhetoric or heat and I don't know if you can convince some congressmen this way. His statement does seem to promise that Bradley will have some pungent detail to present. It seems to me personally that MacArthur is a traitor to his country.

What a beautiful day it is—the sun is bright and my little bird is singing. And when you come right down to it, I should be singing a little myself on paper.

You know it is about time for me to throw out a flock of pencils. They are getting short and I detest short pencils. I think I will discard the short ones today as I finish with each one. I take them to Tom who uses them to draw with. To him they are not short pencils. I am really dawdling today when what I want to write is in my head. It is said that many writers talk their books out and so do not write them. I think I am guilty of this to a large extent. I really talk too much about my work and to anyone who will listen. If I would limit my talk to inventions and keep my big mouth shut about work, there would probably be a good deal more work done. The discussions here in the notes are not included in the interdict, for these notes serve me as a kind of arguing ground for the story. For instance, where do I go from the night ride of Samuel. I know what material must go in but the arrangement of it, where one thing starts and where another and their relationships. And even as I write it I know how it is going to go. I must go to the Hamilton place now to balance one family against another and also to show relationships I have only spoken about. I was wrong about the price per foot for digging a well. Samuel would have charged about fifty cents a foot. The price now is $3.25 without casing and $4.25 with casing. Fifty cents would be about right for his time. When you consider that wages were ordinarily a dollar a day, then you can see that fifty cents a foot would be good pay. A well rig man today gets fifteen to 18 dollars a day and uses machinery. So the price is less per man hour than it was then and probably one could buy for 50 cents in 1898 just about what he can for $3.25 now. Well, there's enough.

And I go to work.

May 9, Wednesday

Today is going to be a violently busy day. It is early but I have to break at 10:30 and go to Waverly's school to see her play Queen Elizabeth to Judy Erwin's* Mary. They have been practicing a long time.

The callus on my writing finger is very sore today. I may have to sandpaper it down. It is getting too big.

I shall phone you this but will put it down here also. I have paper for a little less than two weeks' work. If I run out I will howl like a wolf. So it is time for you to get me another book. This one went faster than I thought it would. If I did not waste these pages, of course, I could probably get the whole novel in one book. But I love the prodigality of it. The violent Willy Nilly. Sometimes the old franticness comes back and has to be resisted. There's no hurry. All the time and all the story in the world. I've never been happier so why should I ever finish this book. It can go on and on, maybe never be done.

Gwyn called yesterday to say that Tom had been exposed to mumps and probably has them. I have never had them and am

---

* A classmate of Waverly's, daughter of the actor Stuart Erwin.

naturally a little timid about them. I started on your present yesterday and made good progress but it will take a long time to do. I hope you will like it. If you do not—there isn't a thing in the world you can do about it because you can't burn it and no one else would have it. I guess that is all of day's occupation. Tonight I really should write some letters. I am very behind even to my family. I don't do anything but the book now.

So we come to our day's inspection of the book and we stand it up and take a look at it. Yesterday I did the scene in the Hamilton kitchen which I hope you will enjoy. It was done for color contrast. I think—and I thought very long in bed about it last night—that I had better begin to terminate this section. It would be easy to hold it off indefinitely but my form seems to be calling for a finish. And it seems to me that since the end differs a great deal from the beginning, perhaps it would be well to set the next part in a chapter of its own, lead into it discursively and then pick up the story and carry it through with great simplicity.

I just had a letter from Beth* with lots of details about the family. So much is forgotten and only a little bit peeks through. And what I want this great sprawling book to do is to be like an experience to the reader, so that perhaps after a little while he will not know whether he read it or whether it happened to him.

Yes, I think it is time to wind in the Cathy section. How strange it is and so must be, the animal anomaly.

I have now reached a time of concertioning in this book so that the words seem to almost come of themselves. I will start today with a groping in Cathy's mind again for her possible native reason and ends. The inspection of the strange and the worship of the unearthly. It is time I think for the book to pause for discussion. It has not done that for a long time. I think that is the way I will do it. That way—first a kind of possible analysis and then quick narrative right to the end, explain it first and then do it. And a whole new thing is coming in. Dam it, this book gets longer, not shorter. Everything has pups. I never saw anything like the way it grows. And when this section is finished I am going to jump a few years—about ten years. That will make our first knowledge of the twins at ten. And the story will start all over again just as it did before.

---

* Mrs. E. G. Ainsworth, Steinbeck's sister, lives in Pacific Grove, California, in the house built by their father and remodeled by John when he lived in it himself.

Now sweetly or sadly, good or bad—the day's work is done. It was a discursive day just as I knew it would be. But there was another reason too. This is a personal book and every now and then I have to yank it back to the personal. I want the illusion of time past [passed?] between the happening and the story to keep it from the kind of immediacy I am trying to lose. And at the same time I want it to be believed as a record of a past truth. Does that make sense to you? I understand it but maybe I haven't said it well. Maybe you won't approve of the little tone of elegy that has crept in—as though I were anticipating tragedy for my audience. Well I am. There are no surprises in this book. But I'll bet my reader can't tell what is going to happen. It's a surprising thing and I don't think even you know what is going to happen. When it comes, it will be so methodical, so factual that it should happen under your nose. And all of it has been planted. Every lead is in. I don't think you will be able to find fault with any of its form. But we'll see.

You know the greatest fault finders will be in my family. None of them will agree that I was right about anything. And maybe I'm not. It's as natural as rain that I should have a little pie-shaped piece of reality cut out of the circle of the past and my own.

We went to see Waverly and her friend perform and they did it very well. Waverly's great grandmother died last night. She will be a sad kid when she hears because she loved that one better than the rest and so did Elaine.

I feel a little heady now. It's been a day of super rest and super work. I called you about the pages being nearly gone and I am pretty sure you will bring them. It's a petty thing, I know, but I am nervous without plenty of pages undirtied. And I would be restless without this kind of paper for the book. It would seem out of drawing and out of key.

May 10, Thursday

Pat, if I had the sense that is the natural right of little green turnips, I would not dawdle today but would rip into the book. Unfortunately I do not have that sense. I want to clean my room today and change my tool rack and generally get neat. A kind of anarchy has set in. My things are all over the floor and a general unneatness has taken the place of my ordinary immaculateness.

In two hours I could fix this and probably will. Just then I had a really commercial idea—a real good one. But I'll keep that to myself. That way I won't get into trouble.

I had hoped to finish the first section of the book this week but there is just too much of it. However, I don't think there is any doubt that I will finish it next week. And that will be the first volume or book or whatever you want to call it. Today's little thing is a violent thing but a quietly violent thing. I don't quite know how I am going to get over the struggle I have to. And the feeling of it is so revolting that I have to tone it down in open statement so that what happens is more or less in the reader's mind. Sometimes I can do this. We'll see if I can do it now. I'll have to try. I want a real struggle, a demoniacal struggle in this. And right at this minute I don't know how I am going to do it. Maybe that's why I keep dawdling. Here for the first time I want the audience to see an open thing in Cathy—not covered, not concealed and not secret. Pat, this book is growing so fast that I can't keep up with it. I don't know what I am going to do. I told you that every part of it had pups. That's the trouble. And here is another thing that is almost frightening—the story comes to me as though I were reading it but not in its final form. Then I must take the story I have heard in my ears and set it down. It is a very curious thing and one that is driving me. But meanwhile I don't know that I will ever finish it. It gets larger all the time.

I want to tell you something and let it work in your mind. Maybe I'll discuss it with you tomorrow. But I'll put it down so you can think of it. Elaine has an ex-relative named Hagy,* a very rich Texan. He is far from literary. On his way to the big oil conference in Europe he stopped by and stayed to dinner. Now I know we always get help from amateurs but I want you to think about this. He asked me what I was writing and I said a very long novel. He asked what it was called. I said Salinas Valley. He asked, "What's it about?" I said it's about my county for the last fifty years.

"I think your title's wrong," he said.

"What do you mean?"

"Well," he said, "nobody who doesn't live there is interested in the Salinas Valley. You had the title yourself. Everybody is interested in my county. Call it that. Then they can connect it with their county."

---

* Lawrence Hagy of Amarillo, Texas.

And you know—maybe he makes sense. But since it is not about the whole county—how would "My Valley" be. It's a wonderful-looking title and it has things Hagy doesn't know. It has the personal quality I am trying to put in the book. Think of it before you discard it. It is a wonderful jacket title too. *MY VALLEY*. The balance of letters, two y's and two ll's, and the M balances the V. And it has great warmth and simplicity too. I will like to hear what you think of this.

And now the time has come. To go to work Callou, Callaise.*

Yrs. very sincerely
Manuel Tiburcio Schmaltz (Spanish Prisoner)

Now you see, god dam it—I never got to the birth. I will do it tomorrow. That's what I mean by the book's growing ahead faster than I can keep up with it. But I must get the birth down because if you were as excited about this next scene as I am, and I hope to make you that excited, you would be angry if you couldn't read it for another week. So I will finish it for you—and incidentally for myself. And now I'll have to think all night about how I am going to do it although I think I already know. And it's a technique I think I can use. But we will see whether I can or not. Lord I'm having fun with this book. Do you like the story of the meteor? And are these Hamiltons beginning to be alive for you? I do hope so.

And now I'm going to give my room a thorough turning out and by tomorrow when you see it, it will be beautiful beyond belief.

May 11, Friday

Another week complete after I do my day's stint. A dark and rainy day and one I like. It is cool and the trees look very nice. When I finish I will take the stuff over to you and we will go to look at the doors you have tracked down in spite of the fact that they may not be right at all.

Last night there were strong symptoms of fatigue although I didn't want to stop. And the story ran with me all night. The scene I have to write today and which I may not finish is rather terrible but in a very quiet way. It is a good day and I feel rested.

---

* " 'O frabjous day! Callooh! Callay!' / He chortled in his joy."—Lewis Carroll, "Jabberwocky."

And next week I think I will finish Book 1.* And such is the design of this work that it will be complete. If anything should happen, it could be printed as it is. This gives me a great deal of security satisfaction. It will be about 95,000 words which is long enough and its design is climactic. The three books will be much better but one will be done. Isn't that a good thought? The ending is strange but it is a complete ending. Isn't that good?

What a day it is, almost dark as night and raining very hard. There's no hurry and still I feel I should hurry. If I don't meet you at three, it doesn't matter. In that case I will meet you at four. What difference does it make? None whatever. I must get over these little worries. I think the human thrives best when he is a little worried and unhappy and this is implemented with needles in the brain.

Now to the book and today's piece. It is the birth of the twins. It will be recorded without thoughts, only in description and dialogue, like a black-and-white movie. I want it to be very convincing. Maybe I'll finish it today and maybe I won't. I am very independent. But the more I think of it—I am only independent in some ways. That's funny, isn't it. Maybe I have a little monster blood in me. I have been told that and sometimes I believe it.

Oh! what a day, so black, so damp and dour. It sets my stage although it was a sunny day when the twins were born; there were no portents unless the pleasantness of the day itself is a portent. I wish I would get to it now. I am ready and the words are beginning to well up and come crawling down my pencil and drip on the paper. And I am filled with excitement as though this were a real birth.

Now I warn you—in this section you will see and hear some strange things. And now I will get into it and may the words be very clean and sharp like good knives.

May 13, Sunday

No, I am not going to do any work today but it does seem strange not to be working. And if I am not careful I might do some of it.

---

* Already Part Two. In the final arrangement of the novel there were four parts instead of three as planned.

May 14, Monday

There is in the air about a man a kind of congealed jealousy. Only let him say he will do something and that whole mechanism goes to work to stop him. The Greeks worked this out to their satisfaction. Jealous gods always present. I am at war with them today. A bug is working in my stomach and chest trying to stop me. I am fighting back because I have not time to enjoy the bug. Maybe I'll win and maybe the bug will win. But he will have to be a strong bug because his natural allies the treacherous Psychos are remaining loyal to me. No fifth column for the bug.

Saturday night I wrote a poem. I'll set it down and you can brush up the lines as you wish. "Gen MacArthur had a fathur two grades above human. In Heaven, he is a Seven Star Angel. And if we wait, Doug will have eight." End of poem—end of era.

You know, Pat, there are times when our thoughts are large and good and full and then there are other times when our thoughts and feelings are small and mean and nervous. Or am I alone in this. This morning I am amazed at the utterly despicable quality of my thinking. And these are just as definitely a part of me as the thoughts of which I can approve. It doesn't do any good to deny such thoughts. I think they turn to poison and sink in if we do. Better to think them through and so lose them. Who knows but what this is the bug's method of making me sick. I hope my work can be good today. I know it will be hard and will take long because a part of my energy will have to be displayed in the battle of staying well. So I won't be able to throw the whole weight on the paper. But I will try. That's the best I can do.

Monday, Monday—the gateway of the week. I can remember Monday in Salinas. How I hated it! My will toward death was very great when I was growing up. I remember the screened window of my room looking out on grey fog and beyond that a grey school and a grey week—and I hated having to pass that gateway into the week. It is not so now. I look forward to Mondays. The death wish is not so strong as it used to be and maybe some time it will disappear entirely. Or maybe this is too much to hope for.

You know I think I am winning. A little shuddery surge of joy just ran over me like a chill. I think the bug is weakening. I think I will kick the shit out of him. Yes, I think I will.

The work today is still reporting and will continue to be all week. You see this is the week when I hope to bring the first book to a close. I think it will be this week. Maybe not because a great deal has to happen yet it will come as it comes. Oh! but I am sluggish and slow today. But I learned long ago that you cannot tell how you will end by how you start. I just glanced up this page for instance. Look at the writing at the top—ragged and angular with pencils breaking in every line, measured as a laboratory rat and torn with nerves and fear. And just half an hour later it has smoothed out and changed considerably for the better. I guess that is the best justification of these notes. They get all or most of the kinks out before I start with the book.

What do you think of the new title now? Do you think it would be injured by that other title, How Green Was My Valley? I don't. But I want you to. Also I want you to review titles to see whether it has ever been used—but if I know you, you have done that already.

And now, finally I am ready for work.

May 15, Tuesday

Last night, we drank our coffee sedately. Talked, listened to a Rubenstein rendition of the Appassionata, went to bed. Read a while and turned out the light. Didn't sleep a single moment. Got up at five, went down to the kitchen, made coffee and since six I have been at this desk. Now if you can tell me why I do that, I will be glad. I felt fine, was tired, even sleepy, no tension, don't miss the sleep a bit. In fact I feel I have somehow found a day. But why this happens fairly often I don't know. There's no sense in it. Insomniacs are supposed to worry, so I can't be one of those. In the very early dawn, I felt a fiendish desire to take my electric pencil sharpener apart. It has not been working very well and besides I have always wanted to look at the inside of it. So I did and found that certain misadjustments had been made at the factory. I corrected them, cleaned the machine, oiled it and now it works perfectly for the first time since I have it. There is one reward for not sleeping.

I am going to make one more attempt to get the other type-script from you. I will be kind and understanding and a little stupid as is expected of me, but if these approaches do not work I shall, by a metamorphosis so quick as to be invisible, turn into a scheming, conniving, murderous fiend. First, my kind side—as you bring the one copy, it must be turned over to Elizabeth because she is going over it with a view to first serial rights which I am told are exempt.* Besides, she feels that a number of short complete sequences may be removed and sold. This means money and nearly two years before anything can be realized on the book. Money means food and security and presents and all of these are the foundation on which happiness may possibly pitch its tent. Now, since the script goes immediately, my dear wife Elaine has never had a chance to read it. So please—for sweet charity's sake, bring me the other typescript. You don't need it yet and I am going to have to have a correction copy. Now there you have my lovely and reasonable side, but if you think you are going to set your aesthetic ass on that copy, you are nuts. Fork it over! You will not have many more warnings and then—Whamo—the sky will fall on you—signed *A Friend*.

Now, although it is still very early, I shall get to the book. You don't like the title MY VALLEY. I have never been a title man. I don't give a dam what it is called. I would call it Valley to the Sea which is a quotation from absolutely nothing but has two great words and a direction. What do you think of that? And I'm not going to think about it any more.

Now yesterday's work—the end of the birth is done. And I wonder if you will have noticed the incredible details about human birth. I wonder on the other hand whether you will have noticed that you furnished every one of those details yourself. I've given you only people and their reactions. But if I have done it well enough you have actually seen the double birth in your own mind. No detail is written. I think it is pretty good and I hope the sense of danger got into it. The real foreboding should rest on it like a crow on a fence. And I am going to have to change tempo now. Today it starts swinging into the end. It will move fast now. It has to reach its climax. And I don't know why I fool around with this when I could be working on it and by god I will. I am peculiarly dangerous today.

May 16, Wednesday

I gabbed to you so much yesterday that I haven't much to say today in the notes. Slept so hard last night that I find it very

---

* I.e., handled by the agent, not by the book publisher.

difficult to wake up this morning. But I will eventually. And I am tired today. Maybe the little change over the week end will be good for me.

I think the book is going to take two more days. I must say I don't feel much up to it today but I will do it. Today's work is mostly dialogue. And some very curious dialogue. I hope I can do it. I wonder where my energy has gone so suddenly. It just departed. But I am sure it will be back. It always is. But I just can't seem to get awake. Then too there is excitement in the house because the new piano is coming this morning. Thank God I can't play or I would never get back to work.

I think I had better forgo any notes today and simply get to my work.

Later. Well I finished my work and it is *not* going to be done tomorrow I don't think. There's a lot more questioning in the first interrogation and then a scene with the deputy and Samuel. Then a final scene with sheriff and deputy. Samuel and Adam. Maybe I can't even finish it this week. The dam thing grows so much. And it has such subtleties.

May 17, Thursday

I am not going to finish the book today, Pat. There are three scenes and all of them are important and long. So I am afraid I won't be able to close the books on this one this week. I'll talk to you about this later today since you will have to come over for the mss. on Friday and maybe about noon. Some little worries coming up. [. . .] Tom is in trouble in school again [. . .] I find it difficult to concentrate when this other thing is hanging. [. . .] It is a tough problem. And I had better get off it now. It can root out all the work and take over [. . .]. You see it has got me running my sentences.

Now I will force myself back to the book and see whether or not I have any self discipline. Maybe it's the darkness before day—who knows.

Now do you wonder why I have all this questioning? Does it interest you? It has a very definite purpose, you know. I don't think I will set down that purpose because you will surely be aware of it. I wish I could have it without other complications but apparently I can't. And maybe I wouldn't be any good at it if I could.

May 18, Friday

Another week going. And how they do go. 120 pages today. Little by little it builds and you can't hardly tell how or when it does it. We go north tonight but not until late so I have plenty of time and I won't have to rush at all. Grey and overcast today and the heat broken. And I am just a little weary. Some things have happened which I won't even bother to put in these notes, but I have had to work with split attention this week and that is always hard for me. I'm not much good at it. I don't do either well I guess, but on the other hand I think the work yesterday was good. It was dialogue which sounded like talk and every bit of it developed the story. I read it over and it is all right. Now today I have two scenes if I am to finish the section. I'm not going to talk about them here because both of them are pretty delicate and I would rather they went down straight. You can see whether you like them. But I don't know whether I will get them both done today.

I wonder whether it will be as hard getting into the next part as it was in this. I hope not. The work rhythm is established anyway. But the book will have to change as the times change. Oh! it's going to be fun—a veritable welter of virtuosity.

The weather has completely changed. The heat is gone for the time being anyway and it is delightfully cool. And now it is time for me to go to work while I can. I have wasted enough time and this morning I have really wasted it and no fooling—wasted it in kind of daydreaming, sometimes a profitable matter but not this time. So I think I had better just turn over the page and start to it.

Today's work will start with a short description of the sheriff which I haven't got yet. So I will leave a space for it.

Well, there is Part I finished. And I hope you like it. I don't know what you'll make of it or what mood it will leave you in. I know the one I want but I can't tell whether this will do it. Anyway there it is. I'm not tired. But I'm very glad the book is not finished—I would hate to have it done. I don't like to think of the time when it is done. That will be a bad day for me. A real bad day. Now I'll spray this week's work and do some little doodling.

May 22, Tuesday

Now, Pat, we come to the second part of the book. Yesterday I did not work. I had a sore left arm which gave me hell. Today it is gone. What strange aches we get, physical resentments against living I guess. You know, I like to think that I am general enough and common enough so that I have some empathetic approach to nearly every human emotion and feeling and thought. Of course it is only that I like to think this. It does not make it true but if it were true I would be a better writer for it. There is one field of feeling, however, in which either I am different from most people or they do not tell the truth—perhaps not knowing it or not daring to face it or perhaps feeling that it is a monstrous thing which should not be brought into the light. I don't know that this is so, I simply offer these as reasons why people do not seem to feel as I do. I refer to the will to live. I have very little of it. This must not be confused with a death wish. I have no will to die but I can remember no time from earliest childhood until this morning when I would not have preferred never to have existed. No moment of joy or excitement or sharp experience of pain or sorrow has even made me want to be alive if the opposite were possible. You see it is no longing for death but a kind of hunger never to have lived. The few times I have stated this I have been attacked with everything from straight disbelief to a kind of hatred as though I were a traitor to life. And perhaps I am. But my feeling is not based on any thought whatever. It lies far below the lighted levels of thought, somewhere in the blackness from which impulses arise. This feeling has its corollary in another which is equally disbelieved and yet is equally true. Having little will to be alive I have also very little personal ego—some vanity but little ego. The two oldest and strongest children of ego are domination and possessiveness, and I have very little of either of these. And the youngest and stupidest child is desire for immortality and I have none of this whatever. Another offspring is competitiveness, which is I guess a desire to prove superiority, and I have none of this either. It is a kind of crippled quality I guess, or perhaps one human characteristic is left out. But what I say is true. To that extent I am a monster like Cathy. And it is strange that my trade is one which usually is chosen by people who have a will both for life and for immortality. That is a paradox I know. I truly do not care about a book once it is finished. Any money or fame that results has no connection in my feeling with the book. The book dies a real death for me when I write the last word. I have a little sorrow and then go on to a new book which is alive. The line of my books on the shelf are to me like very well embalmed corpses. They are neither alive nor mine. I have no sorrow for them because I have forgotten them, forgotten in its truest sense.

Now that I have set down part one of this book it is dead. But fortunately Part II is here to take its place so I do not have the usual quick sorrow. And this is one book during which I will have to resurrect the dead. It is very odd and a new experience to me. I am up early today and I have a whole full free day and many sharpened pencils. Only one thing must be done today and I don't want to discuss that in these notes. But out of that thing must arise how I will feel for a long time to come. It concerns my boys and I think you know how, so I will not write it here lest they might some day read it and be saddened. And they will have sadness enough as they go along. Outside of that the day is made to start Part II. It is a lovely day, bright with sun and the beginning warmth of summer is in the air—so much so that I am thinking of bringing up my cooler and installing it. The time has almost come for that. It will be a frightful job getting it up, and I am not sure that I can do it alone. I can only try and call for help if I find it impossible. But I am immensely strong when I want to be and very, very weak when the will is not in me.

Yesterday I felt weak and frightened at the thought of Part II. But today all that is gone and only a good calmness has taken its place. Perhaps that is because yesterday I thought of it as an immense whole and today my mind is on its opening.

I thought about the book a great deal yesterday—what it is about and what its title should be. It is not local. It is not primarily about the Salinas Valley nor local people. Therefore it should have a general title. Now—its framework roots from that powerful, profound and perplexing story in Genesis of Cain and Abel. There is much of it that I don't understand. Furthermore it is very short, but this story with its implications has made a deeper mark in people than any other save possibly the story of the Tree of Life and original sin. Now since this is indeed my frame—is there any reason to conceal it from my reader? Would it not be better to let him know even in the title what the story is about? With this in mind I went back to Genesis. I do not want a direct quotation but if I can find a symbol there which is understood on sight and which strikes deep, I will have my title. The punishment of Cain is a strange and perplexing one. Out of Eve's sin came love and death. Cain invented murder and he is punished by life and protection. The mark put on him is not placed there to punish him but to protect him. Have you ever thought of that? And this is the best known mark in the world. So I suggest as a title for my book Cain Sign. It is not a direct quote, it is short, harsh, memorable and nearly everyone in the world knows what it means. And it is a pretty good-looking title too. What do you think of it?

And now I guess I have written enough notes for today and I will go to work on Part II

May 23, Wednesday

The joyful thought came to me this morning that you may be getting god dam sick of this endless soapbox and there is not a thing in the world you can do about it. You are sunk. The one thing you can do is not to read it and I think you are too curious for that so I have you and I can be as dull as I wish. Ho! Ho!

You will have noticed that this section is pretty beat up. It happened this way. Last night I took the day's work to bed to read to Elaine and I spilled a glass of water on it. So I dried it off and I am going to use it. The last half of 123 is a little rocky but it is better than breaking the sequence. Now—I have sketched in the background history of the Valley in the 1900s. With so much to be written sometimes it is difficult to know where to put what. The matter of arrangement can be very important indeed. But I thought about it a good deal last night when I didn't sleep much and I think I know what comes next. And it must be extremely well done and again underwritten. Summer being comen in and this morning I brought up my air conditioner and when I finish work today I will build the bracket to hold it and tomorrow morning I will mount it and then I will be fixed for the summer.

Now—I guess that is about enough. I think you will be delighted over the episode of the naming of the twins. I am. Now I'll let you know and let you go.

May 24, Thursday

Another week pinching off. Today I have those meaningless apprehensions that come out of the ground, go nowhere, mean nothing and disappear—what I have called Welsh rats in the book. We will have a fine time on the island this summer but sometimes I wish I didn't have to move at all until my book is done. However, that is only some times. Yep! I've got the Welsh rats but I have all day to get my work done, barring a few accidents which might happen.

On Saturday and Sunday instead of stopping writing, I want to do a short story that is on my mind. Unless I write it I will be bothered by it. It is just as well to get such a thing out of my mind. So I will do it and get a lot of things said that should be said and should be said by me— The wind is howling in turret and tree.

It's a wild day outside, Pat. A little of winter looking back. I love the winter. I must have had good winters—better than summers. This book is doing remarkable things to and for me. My memory is sharpened and tightened and sometimes the feel of words is like a round and warm emotion. It is impossible to describe the feeling but it is like a party feeling and good like afternoon feeling.

I should not dawdle too much today. It would be better to go directly to my work and trap my Welsh rats. Otherwise they may give me trouble. The day is still quite young and quite desirable. I should really go to work now. I read in the Saturday Review about how I am writing this book. It is called ambitious and I guess it is. Any long book is bound to be an ambitious book. Also in the same edition an article by Harold*—very clear and precise and not exactly happy in its conclusions. It makes me wonder whether anything has ever been happy while it was happening. Oh now to work—my god! To work.

May 25, Friday

Today the last day of the book week. The story is jumping along in my head. I could go on without stopping now. I worked and studied and made research until about 3 last night. I have my material all ready now and I must say it is one of the most devilish plans I have ever heard of. Absolutely devilish. And the awful thing is that it would work. That is the really terrible thing. Thank goodness I am not a criminal or am I just thinking it? I sometimes wonder if I must not be all the people I am writing about. And good lord there are so many I must be hundreds.

---

* Harold Guinzburg's article in the *Saturday Review*, May 26, 1951, was entitled "Book Publishing: A Dubious Utopia."

I will finish my work and then I think I will meet you at your office or somewhere near there. I want you to look at something. I think you would like to do that. Also I must get a rubber stamp made for forwarding mail this summer. It is a fine brilliant day today. Sun beautiful. I shall be anxious to hear how you like the opening of the second part. I think it is pretty good and so does Elaine. Trying to get Gwyn on the phone but it is always busy. [. . .] It is getting late and I haven't started my work yet. Trying to get that call through before I go to work.

May 28, Monday

By some chicanery it has become Monday. You don't dare turn your back anymore. I found it difficult to awaken this morning and am not yet awake completely. I worked over the week end and got no rest. Maybe that is the reason—worked on a short story. But maybe not—perhaps I am just lazy today. I think you enjoyed going out to see the surprise*—didn't you? I still don't know how I am going to swing it but I will—some way. I think it is a good investment. I'm sure of that.

A good morning. It is I who am not good. I am sluggish. Must shake that off because today's work is very important. Oh the next few days are such careful work to do. It must be very ingeniously done. Kate is going to do an ingenious thing and I must underwrite it to make it convincing. I must do it with straight description so that one thing follows another. It is strange and good that I never come to this book with reluctance—often with terror, but I have never since I started writing it wished I were not writing it—not even for a second.

Today the air smells like Monday and the traffic in the street is like Monday. It is really a Monday kind of a day. I wish I had the last page of mss. I made a couple of notes at the top of the page but I would like to review a few lines of dialogue. But I guess it will be all right. I guess it will be all right. But it is such a delicate little scene that I want to make it very good and very very convincing. And it's a pretty hellish scene. I think of nothing like it in literature. Surely I didn't steal it. I wonder where I got it. Only a few time elements to work out. And exact minute-to-minute happenings.

I should get to it pretty soon. I can hear it and see it in my head just the way it happened. I know why I am making so much

---

* A boat; see page 110.

of it. This scene is going to balance the next. And it must have some pretty powerful matter in it to do that. The wind is blowing over me too much.

May 29, Tuesday

I did not wake up on time this morning. It was clock business. When I depend on a clock to ring I am in trouble. I awakened, saw it was not 7 and went back to sleep. Well the clock was not running. This makes me irritable. I hate such interference. And my work will take much longer today because I am irritable. A dark day clouded and brooding. Elizabeth Otis and I figured out my numbers of words yesterday and it is not nearly as many as I had thought. I am glad of that because I don't want this book to be too bulky. It takes 400 typed pages to make a hundred thousand words and I haven't even got that many yet. Now—let's see where we have got—discipline! god damn it, discipline! I do hate these indisciplines which throw me back. Today I guess I must work very slowly. It is a frightening thing I have to write. Detailed and sharp but almost in a monotone. If I can write the next series of scenes and their culmination, I think I can write anything. But as I told you yesterday, I feel a little guilty for having thought the scenes at all. But that is the way it is. My god what a strange grey day. And having overslept I have a kind of a grey mind.

Tonight we are going to the second opening of Oklahoma. Nine years ago Elaine opened it the first time in New York. So we can't afford not to go tonight. So many things to think and to do. It is requiring great will power to pull back to the book. Thank goodness it is not a dull book. I would never get back to it. It is time for me to go to work but first I will feed and water my bird.

There, he is fed with ground carrots and mockingbird food. And he has a bowl of water to bathe in. You would think he would be happy. But I suppose he is not. Who can tell. It is a preverse human attitude to imagine that birds sing when they are happy. Humans do not—humans sing most beautifully in pain and longing. And a bird usually sings for love but love wanted and expected. Give a male bird a female and he ceases to sing. I draw no conclusion whatever from this. And isn't it odd. People very rarely sing for joy.

Now the time has come and I must go to work.

May 30, Wednesday, Memorial Day

I'm having one hell of a time today. I'm tired, so tired. It has come up like a wall. Nearly always I can fake it with simple will but I don't know whether I can make it today or not. I know dammed well I will finish the episode today and then maybe I will go to bed. I'm just pooped. I have to get to it and see if I can operate. Two years ago last night I met Elaine for the first time. Memorial Day is our anniversary. And what changes there have been. I did not expect to survive then and I don't think I would have. Every life force was shriveling. Work was non-existent. I remember it very well. The wounds were gangrenous and mostly I just didn't give a dam. Now two years later I have a new life and a direction. Accidents can be benign. I am doing work I like.

It is a really beautiful day. And maybe I will awaken pretty soon. I don't want *not* to work and yet I don't seem to get to it. The method—it is the method that is so dreadful. There is one thing I eliminated and I think it has to go back. Maybe in the form of an inset. Yes, it has to go in. Otherwise there isn't a real and understandable point. I could understand it myself and maybe you could but I wonder whether our general reader would have such a sense of the under thing unless it is seriously put down. So today I will have to write the inset.

Later. What a complicated animal a human is. I went down and sat in the garden for an hour trying to think myself out of the curious maze I am in. And I think the inset is the answer. Let me try to explain. I am dealing with a process which is part external reality and part mind and soul. In my mind I went over it and worked out every detail. One key detail I threw out and went ahead. Then my engine grinds to a stop and I don't know why. And I think it is because I left out that detail. I am limited here by not being able to go into Kate's mind. I will do this. Therefore she must be made clear by her speech and her actions. And I have made her start a process activated by thought and I haven't even given a hint of what that thought might be. Why did she start the process? I have not made that clear. I'm glad I caught it now because later I might only feel the lack without knowing what it is that is troubling me. And if I can get that in today I will be satisfied with my day's contribution.

It is Memorial Day and people in their new shoes are walking by in the street very proud and jerky in the sun. And curiously enough the power and the glory is flowing back into me. And it's because of the clarity I got in the garden. And the method of clarity.

Now the scene I have to write is not only a degenerate one but it is strong degeneracy feeding on weak degeneracy. It is almost a sickening thing but it has to go in or the rest of the scene or sequence does not make sense. Also the chapter which is to follow has great cleanness and purity but it will not appear so clean if it does not have a contrast.

Do you see what I mean? Well, all right then—I will write the inset.

Later. Now. There's the insert done and it went three hand-written pages. It is horrible but it brings Kate out in the open—the only time it will ever happen. But I think now the sequence is maturated so that there will be no surprise at what she does. It is all in and understandable. And psychiatrically very accurate I might say. Let me know what you think of it. It has taken me all day to write because I was so sluggish about getting started. But I think that this sequence might be one of the most effective pieces of horror in any language. But I don't know and won't know until somebody reads it.

May 31, Thursday

Oh lord, another week is ending up and I haven't got much further. I will complete Kate this week. I don't think I can do it today but maybe I can. It is a thing to try. But unless this is cold and detailed it will not be convincing. It must be set down like a record. Like a report. I think I will put it down like a report. I wonder how I can make it absolutely cold. The work yesterday —the inset—champagne and unmasking was so horrible that it gave me bad dreams myself.* I guess working on the dreams must have done it. But it will be some time before I get over it. And the next sequence will be even more terrible because it is without emotion. This is probably why Kate is so frightening. She has no conscience. It is much the same thing as happened to me during the war when I used to go out to visit the burned British pilots. It wasn't that they had no faces that was horrible; you could get used to the blob of flesh without lips, noses, eyelids or ears. The thing you couldn't get used to was the fact that

---

* Chapter 20.

behind that they were perfectly nice normal men with normal impulses. This was the real horror. And Kate's horror is her lack of human reaction. And also that you don't know what she wants. In the last scene one of her impulses burst through but it was pulled back instantly. Now—today the final process starts and when it starts it will go through to its conclusion. It won't waver anymore and there will be no side issues. This must be the most carefully constructed crime. It must have no loop holes of any kind. And I think I can do that.

Later. Now there, Mr. Pat, if you can untangle these notes, you're good. Just follow the date numbers if you can. As I had hoped, I am going to finish with the whorehouse tomorrow. I will be glad to. It is a tale of such horror that I will be happy to be done with it. But I think it has to be done. And then next week I will get back to the twins and the story will open out again. I think you will find that Cathy as Kate fascinates people though. People are always interested in evil even when they pretend their interest is clinical. And they will mull Kate over. They will forget I said she was bad. And they will hate her because while she is a monster, she is a little piece of the monster in all of us. It won't be because she is foreign that people will be interested but because she is not. That is not cynicism either.

And now I am going to leave this for today. It has been a hard week. Too many other things have been involved—things to be solved. We had to go out two nights. I got too tired. But it will be done tomorrow. Sat. & Sun. I will work again on my short story.

June 1, Friday

Late again because of so many things to be done and to be thought about. I don't think the book is suffering. I'm keeping the two apart. The week is gone now and how did it ever get to be June. I guess you will be coming over for coffee and manuscript this afternoon. Anyway I will call you in a little while. My pencils are getting low and I can't find any in the neighborhood. Maybe you can get some over where you are. I'll ask you to try anyway.

It is hot today but not quite hot enough to turn on air-conditioning. Now I should go right to work and get it done. But I don't know. It is a dawdle day for me and I think my handwriting shows it. Now I will call you and ask you to bring me some money too. So I called and you are not at your desk. I wonder where you are. So now I will go to work and finish up this sequence. And I'll be glad too. Well I finally got you and it's about time too. And now I will be ready to work.

June 4, Monday

Dear Pat. Another Monday. Feeling a little rocky. I worked over the week end on that other story and had to throw it away again. It takes me so long in planning to do the simplest thing. I don't know what will come of that. Bad dreams last night. Dreams of hopeless debt, which of course I do not have but I dreamed I had them which is just as bad. Strange terrible dreams as though I were not doing enough. And I think I am doing all I can. There was a time when I didn't think I had any limitation either qualitative or quantitative. I don't know what I think now. I do know I have a pace and to go beyond it is to waste time rather than to gain it. Sometime I'll try to work out the relation of dawdling to work.

I was interested last Friday in your sense of shock over the end of the Kate story. I had the same sense of shock writing it. I think you were shocked that I could think such things and so I was also. But the fact seems to be that I can think almost anything, which means I suppose that I can be almost anything. But I believe what the sheriff says—that anybody is a murderer if you find the key to his trigger finger. Kate's episode is finished for a while but it is not finished finally. There will be two more episodes with Kate before the book finally closes.

The design of this book, made so long ago, seems to hold. It has a quality now to me of something that has happened so that no protest will change it. My job seems to be to live long enough and strongly enough to set it down. That's funny, isn't it? Strange—this morning my mind is in a state of feud. You just called saying I can't serve two gods. And your remarks make very good sense except for one thing. To a certain extent I must serve two masters—1, the book and 2, the other life. Carried to its extreme I would not be able to make out a grocery list if I were so obsequious to the book. The day is still very young. And I wonder whether I am. Every now and then a kind of sick weariness falls on me. It was so yesterday. It is not being tired but just fed up. This could probably be traced to feeding and yet it would be strange in a world of ups and downs if the human body and mind did not have lumps and hollows. My handwriting this morning is full of lumps and hollows which means usually that I am not yet set in my mind for work. I have word this morning that the boat should be there when we arrive. What fun that is going to be. And I have not told anyone. Anyone at all. Elizabeth, Waverly (because she is going away), and you—are the only ones who know. I am really looking forward to the summer. And I do hope my work can go on. I see no reason why it should not. We will have little or no social life. I will go to work very early and try to get air and swimming and paddling and sailing in the afternoon. My health has been extraordinarily good. And now my handwriting has settled down and so I know it is time for me to go to work. And so I will try.

Later. Now there, Mr. Pat, is the opening. It is designedly slow —has to be to balance the last section. It has to get back to the casual and I am doing it this way on purpose. I hope it doesn't sound dull. But I do want everything to be in balance. If this book were about only one thing it would be different, but it is about everything so it must rock like a star. And so you will find many changes and they will not be accidents—they are designed and each one has its purpose. I am pretty sure you sense these things but I draw them to your attention anyway. Tomorrow comes the theological discussion and the shocking of Adam. You are going to see Samuel in a new light. He could be an active man as well as a passive one and you're going to see activity. So many things going on around. Some time I will tell you a really evil story that is happening to me now. But I think you know what it is.

And that is my work for today.

June 5, Tuesday

Your letter came this morning. Do you know, Pat—I have a curious reactive pattern. I noticed it during the war in combat and I have noticed it in other things as well as in this. Little things can upset me completely with fear or nervousness, or rage. But big things freeze me. My mind goes absolutely cold and then it moves very slowly like a sniffing fox. What you say is very clear. And I search in my own little knowledge and experience. It does not seem to me to be hemorrhage because of a number of things. It does seem to be heart—perhaps. The first thing for me is to find out from someone who knows. And that I am in process of doing. And I will shortly know. This will hit me in the night and suddenly but right now I am frozen and I must know. Then, when I do, you had better guard yourself because if you do not do as I say, you will encounter a savagery you cannot even suspect. Now I will leave it until I know more. And I will very shortly.

Last night I sat late talking with Jean* and Elaine. And on my way to bed I was torn out of my pattern. I never write out of hours. But I came in and wrote the dialogue of Sam'l. Hamilton which is in today's work—it tore out so rapidly that the words are nearly unreadable. It is a completely passionate piece of writing. I knew Sam'l. was going to be violent but I didn't know the quality of his violence. It is very odd—the compulsion.

I have sharpened up a new 12 of pencils, fine long ones. This is a kind of indulgence. How I love a new pencil. And I discarded all the little ones. Tom can use them for his drawings. There's a terrible buzz of frustration in me. I can't find the man I want. I hate waiting.

June 6, Wednesday

Thank God that black Tuesday is over. I could not get to the machine until 5 and I guess if I had not had the discipline of the day's work, I would have climbed the walls. Isn't it strange that I had done the dialogue the night before and for the first time. I'm like Ethel—I'll begin to believe myself if I'm not careful. I slept very badly last night, buzzing like a cheap over-wound clock, but all's good today. I'm going to see the boys late this afternoon and earlier I will buy them bathing suits. And I have a pocket knife and a gun that shoots paper for Johnny's birthday. And tomorrow, if I can get Tom to ask me, I would like to go to his school to observe method. The teacher wants me to go but I wouldn't think of going without his invitation. It would be like snooping. I am going to let him hold the eagles. I think he needs a little eminence. And keeping the flag would be good for him. And there is no eminence like taking care of a responsibility. The eagles of the Xth Legion for instance.

Now—I still have the twinge and creak on my mind but thank heaven now only a pattern and groundless. I don't know

---

* His niece, Jean Ainsworth.

whether I have the poop to write well today. That takes the kind of energy which may have gone for a while. But I can always throw it away and I do have hidden pockets of energy that open up when I need them. I had a good long letter from Beth. Had asked her for some advice about the boys. She is so wise and good. Now my bird is fed and watered and has had his bath. And he is singing very well and cocky. And I should be able to sing also— and maybe will. We can do strange and wonderful things when we want to—or need to. One thing I found out in the war is that I can do nearly anything if the pressure is great enough and nearly nothing without pressure. And could that be the reason why paternalisms fail? Because they remove the necessary pressures on men? I can complain like mad but I never have done good work when there was perfect and uncomplicated ease. Ay Lord! my relief is very great. And I'll now put down a few words.

June 7, Thursday

I'm afraid I kind of pooped out yesterday. The fire went out of me and I stopped in the middle. I guess I'm not as tough as I get to thinking. Went up to see the boys and got their clothes to be sent. Then this morning I went to Tom's school to watch the teaching methods. And I learned quite a lot. I thought it was important that I go. And I can't seem to get hold of myself today. My mind is like a god dammed animal. If it gets out it is very hard to catch. I've had it in chains for quite a long time and now I'll have to get a net over it. It's flying away. I feel like such a fool, but there it is. Maybe I will kick over the tracks today. Maybe fighting it is no good and I should let it ride. The time is late and it will be difficult. I'm being real difficult to myself. I know I'll pick up confidence but I don't have much now. Maybe that would be a good idea. I haven't rested for three weeks now and maybe that is it. I might just be tired.

June 8, Friday

Yesterday was a bust; I suppose the greatest of self-indulgence. I guess this is why I give myself so much time for error. And today is nearly as bad. It makes me suspicious and untrustful of myself. My brain acts like a bad child, willful and sneering. And oh! the tricks I can use to justify it so that in the end it becomes downright virtuous. I guess it's like the necessity for hating the person you have injured. I never feel virtuous unless I have a sense of guilt. I've been nervous this week, sure, but maybe I have used the nervousness as an excuse or maybe the nervousness itself is a self-deceptive device. Today you should be coming over for a week's work and I haven't much to give you. I have been very bad. And this makes me shy. Time creeps on me too in a nightmarish way. I don't think I ever told you this but once in college I went flibberty geblut and got to going to the library and reading what I wanted instead of what was required. I got behind and then I got so far behind that I could not possibly catch up. And I still have bad dreams about that. It must have cut a very deep channel.

Today our library chairs came just a few days before we go away. Isn't that terrible? But it always happens. I am having such trouble this week—it is a sloppy slippery week. My work does not coagulate. It is as unmanageable as a raw egg on the kitchen floor. It makes me crazy. I am really going to try now and I'm afraid that the very force of the trying will take all the life out of the work. I don't know where this pest came from but I know it is not new. Now I'll crack down and

June 11, Monday

If anything gets done in this hysterical week of moving I will be very surprised but then I am fairly consistently surprised by everything. Spent the week end nurturing and complaining about a sick stomach, which was probably what was wrong with me all along. I suspect a little exercise is going to help that along. I haven't had much lately, not even the walking I am accustomed to. I was amused at your reference to the boat the other day. You thought I couldn't keep it [secret] and twice it has been you who have nearly blown it. I guess because it is on my mind and not so much on yours.

I wish I knew how people do good and long-sustained work and still keep all kinds of other lives going—social, economic, etc. I can't. I seem to have to waste time, so much dawdling to so much work. I am frightened by this week before it even happens. If I had any sense I would leave my book this week. But that would not be good because it would divorce me from its rhythm and it would take too long to come back to it. So I'll simply get as much done as I can and work as long as is feasible.

Tomorrow is Johnny's birthday. I'll have to go up early with his presents. There are very few this year. I want to get them out of the awful material thing that is so constantly around them. If they can survive that, it will be fine. Just now they think in terms of things almost exclusively. Another thing given them too deeply is "mine-thine" but mostly mine. I'll see what I can do this summer. If I can do one fifth of the things I want to this summer, it will be wonderful.

The day progresses and so does my stomach. I think I am about ready to start on the old trail again. My mind is not as crystal clear as I could wish it. I slept too long and too hard over the week end. My greatest fault, at least to me, is my lack of ability for relaxation. I do not remember ever having been relaxed in my whole life. Even in sleep I am tight and restless and I awaken so quickly at any change or sound. It is not a good thing. It would be fine to relax. I think I got this through my father. I remember his restlessness. It sometimes filled the house to a howling although he did not speak often. He was a singularly silent man—first I suppose because he had few words and second because he had no one to say them to. He was strong rather than profound. Cleverness only confused him—and this is interesting —he had no ear for music whatever. Patterns of music were meaningless to him. I often wonder about him. In my struggle to be a writer, it was he who supported and backed me and explained me—not my mother. She wanted me desperately to be something decent like a banker. She would have liked me to be a successful writer like Tarkington but this she didn't believe I could do. But my father wanted me to be myself. Isn't that odd. He admired anyone who laid down his line and followed it undeflected to the end. I think this was because he abandoned his star in little duties and let his head go under in the swirl of family and money and responsibility. To be anything pure requires an arrogance he did not have, and a selfishness he could not bring himself to assume. He was a man intensely disappointed in himself. And I think he liked the complete ruthlessness of my design to be a writer in spite of mother and hell. Anyway he was the encourager. Mother always thought I would get over it and come to my senses. And the failure of all the Hamiltons might be that they came to their senses. And now I have spewed enough and I will go to work.

There's my word rate done but I think I will go on. I lost so much time last week that it would do no harm to do more this week. It might soften my conscience. And if you wonder why I am spending so much time on this naming—you must know that I am stating my thesis and laying it out. And I am glad that I can use the oldest story in the world to be the design of the newest story for me. The lack of change in the world is the thing which astonishes me. So I am going to let these three men go over the old story and illuminate it, each one out of his own experience. And you will tell me if I do well.

Still the same day. And now I had set down in my own hand the 16 verses of Cain and Abel and the story changes with flashing lights when you write it down. And I think I have a title at last, a beautiful title, *EAST OF EDEN*. And read the 16th verse to find it. And the Salinas Valley is surely East of Eden. I could go on and write another page and perhaps it would be good, who knows. Or maybe not. What a strange story it is and how it haunts one. I have dreaded getting into this section because I knew what the complications were likely to be. And they weren't less but more because as I went into the story more deeply I began to realize that without this story—or rather a sense of it—psychiatrists would have nothing to do. In other words this one story is the basis of all human neurosis—and if you take the fall along with it, you have the total of the psychic troubles that can happen to a human. I am not going to write any more today but maybe tomorrow I can do a little more.

June 12 [TUESDAY]

Restless night full of thoughts. We went to Elizabeth's to dinner and had a good talk. But I do find it very hard to lose the work when it has run so hard. And my discovery of yesterday is sure burning in me. I have finally I think found a key to the story. The only one that has ever satisfied me. I think I know about the story finally after all this time. It is a fascinating story and my analysis which is going in today should interest you. It should interest scholars and it should interest psychiatrists. Anyway at the risk of being boring I'm going to put it all in today. And it will only be boring to people who want to get on with the plot. The reader I want will find the whole book illuminated by the discussion: just as I am. And if this were just a discussion of

Biblical lore, I would throw it out but it is not. It is using the Biblical story as a measure of ourselves.*

Well there's the naming and if you are interested, you can find a great deal in it. It is a hard thing to do. And I could have put it in a kind of an essay but I think it was better to let it come out of these three. And the writing of it has exhausted me. I planned to write another page today. But it's the end.

June 18, Monday

Dear Pat—: I thought I would lose a week in moving but it seems to me that maybe I won't. It is Monday and I am going to try to start to work. I have little hope of reestablishing the working rhythm the first day but at least I am trying. This is a beautiful place † and the most peaceful I have ever seen. The boys are good, the weather cool, and if I can't work it will be because of what we talked about—things are too good. But I will try. You can see that my handwriting is a little haywire yet. So I will have to dawdle until it settles down. Change of desk has something to do with it I guess. I have a little room to work in and it is mine exclusively and I can look at the ocean out of my window. It has a desk to work on—not a tilting desk but an ordinary one. I will soon get used to that, I think. The question is one of rhythm. After a break, it takes time to get it moving in waves again. But that is simply a matter of keeping at it.

I won't try to describe it here because you will be seeing it and I need my descriptive time. The work day will be like this: Up at 7:30 all of us. To work at 8:30. Elaine and the boys will go to the beach mostly taking their lunch. I will work until I have finished. Then we will go to other beaches, go fishing, swimming, sailing or what have you. To bed very early after dining, etc.

It is a matter of sorrow to me that my disposition went to pieces in the move. I think this was largely because of the break in work and the change. It will improve as the work starts. And now I think it might be time to start with the Nantucket section of the work. It will be interesting to see whether there is any change in tone to match the place. I don't think there will be. But we shall see.

Now—for plan. The next chapter will be the life of Tom

---

* Chapter 22 [4].
† Siasconset on Nantucket Island, off the coast of Massachusetts.

Hamilton. It will be fairly long and I shall be thinking that ten years are passing. So that when the next chapter starts, the boys will be ten years old. Then the story will move up in time very rapidly to their seventeenth year. And that will be the critical year of their lives, particularly Aaron's life. So now I start. But first I must get a glass to hold my pencils.

June 19, Tuesday

Well, oddly enough the work went well yesterday—very concentrated as it should be and moving in toward something. I think I have a large key. I did not sleep last night and I look forward to those nights of discovery. I have one about once a week. And after everyone is asleep there is such quiet and peace, and it is during this time that I can explore every land and trail of thinking. Conjecture. Sometime I will tell you about this in detail if you are interested. I split myself into three people. I know what they look like. One speculates and one criticises and the third tries to correlate. It usually turns out to be a fight but out of it comes the whole week's work. And it is carried on in my mind in dialogue. It's an odd experience. Under certain circumstances it might be one of those schizophrenic symptoms but as a working technique, I do not think it is bad at all.

I'm getting into Tom Hamilton today, and he is a strange man, shy and silent, and good—very good and confused. I don't think he ever knew what was wrong with him. But he bears out the thesis of guilt—carries it to its logical conclusion so that he must sacrifice himself. And his sacrifice was strange and rather sweet. I guess the Hamiltons were all nuts, just as my father said. And now to work on Tom.

June 20, Wednesday

And a beautiful day. I am deep in Tom now. Last night I dreamed a long dream of my own paralysis and death. It was objective and not at all sad, only interesting. I'm pretty sure this was set off by the study of Tom Hamilton. I hope you will like the study of Tom. It is very close and I think very true and also it is very important to our story. It is one of the keys to the story and the story attempts to be a kind of key to living. It is a fascination to me to dig up all of these old things and try to re-evaluate them in the light of my greater age. Curious things come out. All yesterday's work about Mary trying to get to be a boy is true to the smallest detail. It came up in my memory as I was working. This island is wonderful. I feel at home here. I wonder if it is my small amount (¼) of my New England blood operating. The people here do not consider me a stranger and we seem to recognise each other. It is a pleasant island but there is energy here too. I have no impulse to neglect my work. In fact I never felt better about working. I am going to ask you to get some books for me. But I will put that in a letter. I got plastic spray so all of this stuff which will go to you Saturday will be well sprayed and preserved. It is necessary because of the dampness here.

And now to work.

June 21, Thursday

The first week two thirds over. Up early and Elaine took the boys to a picnic at the beach. Will come back for me at 2 P.M. when I hope to have finished my work. But I am dawdly today. I seem to waste time—to find many little things to do. I am determined not to let down my quota even if I have to work at night—and here's a curious thing. If you are determined to finish even if you work at night, you usually find that you don't have to work at night.

I was pleased to get your wire that the Ricketts had signed.* They could have caused great trouble simply by doing nothing. I'll bet you are relieved. You letter was good and I liked it. It is strange not to be able to discuss things regularly. And with me too—East of Eden grows as the final title. I wonder whether you ought to try it on anyone else, though, before they know what the book is about. It sounds like a soft title and it is anything but soft. Once you get it in your mind, it fastens. I think the quotation "And Cain etc." should be at the bottom of the title page and in fairly large italics—maybe even with the pronouncing spacing between the letters. There should never be any doubt in the reader's mind what the title refers to.

Your new translation of the story has one most important change. It is the third version. The King James says of sin crouching at the door, "Thou shalt rule over it." The American Standard says, "Do thou rule over it." Now this new translation says,

---

* As Edward F. Ricketts had died, the approval of his estate was required for separate publication of Steinbeck's narrative text from Sea of Cortez. See footnote on page 28.

"Thou *mayest* rule over it." This is the most vital difference. The first two are 1, a prophecy and 2, an order, but 3 is the offering of free will. Here is individual responsibility and the invention of conscience. You can if you will but it is up to you. I would like to check that phrase over. Will you do it for me? The exact word—because if it is incontrovertibly, "thou mayest" I must put this in my discussion, because it will turn out to be one of the most important mistranslations in the Old Testament. Get me the Hebrew word, will you? The word that has been variously translated "do thou," "thou shalt," and "thou mayest." This is important. This little story turns out to be one of the most profound in the world. I always felt it was but now I know it is. Now there is one other thing. Abel brought of the firstlings of the flock and the *fat thereof*. I know that the animals were brought to the altar alive and that the fires were usually made with the fat. But does this mean 1, that firstlings were fat? 2, does it mean that both firstlings and mature animals were brought or does fat simply refer to goodness like the fat of the land? One other thing occurs to me. What does firstling mean? We have thought it meant the young lambs like firstlings of the year. But the words say firstlings of the flock, and might this not mean the best of the flock, in which case fat would simply be a repetition of the meaning *best*. Fat would refer to the *flock* and not the animals. There—I've given you a lot to do for me but I think it is work you will not dislike. And when we finish we will be authorities on this story. If firstling and fat are qualitative, then fruit of the earth without a qualitative might be some key to the rejection. Now—I must get to my work.

Later. There I have finished my day's work. And I think you can see where this section is going.

June 22, Friday

Last day of the first working week at Siasconset and I think a pretty good week. I'll have to wait to see what you think about it. If I finish in time I will send you the week's work tonight and it will be there Monday morning sure as shooting. As this mss. will tell you, it is very damp here. Stamps stick together. I am glad I am spraying the paper now. Even the pencils seem softer in the dampness. But the air is cool and lovely and the sun is warm. The boat has still not arrived. Isn't that crazy. Can't imagine what has happened unless the man just didn't send it. I should have done it myself I guess.

I hope you will like the family meeting of yesterday's work. I think it was pretty much the way they used to happen. They were a high-strung bunch, the Hamiltons. My father used to say affectionately that they were all crazy. And I guess they were and I guess I am. I feel so some of the time anyway.

The mornings are heavy with fog and then about ten o'clock the sun burns through and it gets warm and lovely and the breeze blows sweet and cool. If you want to be hot, you just get out of the wind. This day is going just that way. And a little gurgle of joy is starting in my stomach that means I am going to like working today. This dam book does go on and on. And today is going to happen just what you knew was going to happen. I want to give it a curious feeling of farewell without ever saying it. I want to make it funny that you can't laugh at. Let's see if I can do it. This is the last time you will see Samuel Hamilton except on his death and I'm not sure you will see him then. I have spoken of his death very early in the book. It occurs to me that it might be better to let it go at that. He lived a very short time after he left the ranch and nothing important to this book happened afterwards, but the work of today and perhaps one more day is very important because I hope I am going to show you Samuel in a kind of golden light, the way such a man should be remembered.

Now in the work today or tomorrow I am going to need that Hebrew word which has been variously translated "do thou," "thou shalt," and "thou mayest." I need the word and I want you to get me a good scholarly discussion of it. I have a charming scene to use it in and I can write it all only leaving out that one word to be filled in later.*

Do you feel that this book is holding up? It is hard for me to know. I think it is but I am deeply immersed in it. The trouble is that you are deeply immersed in it too. And I wonder whether you have been able to keep a detached attitude. Elizabeth has the kind of criticism that can snap apart from any personality. But tell me, have you ever been this closely associated with a book before? While it was being written, I mean. I don't think you have but perhaps.

Now I will say good-bye for this week and get to work. This

* The word was "timshel." See page 122. The Hebrew characters were carved under the title on the cover of the box that Steinbeck was making for Covici.

afternoon, Friday, I will mail the ten pages airmail registered. And I am sure you will have them by Monday. And I know that you will let me know that they have arrived. We may get a phone next week and if we do, I will call you one day just to hear your voice. Now I want you to go back to Juan Negrin. It may be that he will want to increase the strength of the medicine a little. Only two is not bad but I think it can be arranged so that there are not any. It is remarkable, isn't it. But then he is a remarkable man and I am fond of him. Lord, I have good friends, such good and great friends.

Now there you have it. And I wonder if it has possibly the little perfume I wanted it to have. On Monday Samuel will visit Adam Trask and the twins and Lee again and that will be the last of him. But he must leave a light (as the litany says), to lighten the gentiles.

And that's all now. You'll have ten more pages next week.

June 25, Monday

Dear Pat. I get the feeling that since I have put things in these notes, I have written them to you. I am going to phone you this morning on our new phone and also to let you know that we have one. Also to tell you that the boat arrived and to tell you that the boat arrived yesterday, so you won't assault the man at the factory. I wonder why it was so late but am very glad it came at all. We set up the boat and painted it and if we can, we will put it in the water this afternoon. It is a very pretty thing.

I fell to pieces this week end—got full of congestions and aches that I couldn't shake. Horrible dreams and many aches. I think just a very bad cold with nervousness. The boys have a transition to make and so do we. Ordinarily I have two complete lives to lead, book life and other and now I have three. And I do not change very easily. I get into the most trouble when I am not working actively. But that is always so. Tom needs camp very badly. He needs the supervision of older boys. In many ways he is a baby—less old than he should be. This grows from a frantic desire to be appreciated. He tries to be like Catbird. And like most humans, some of his methods of attracting attention are pretty unattractive and nerve-wracking.

This may be a bad week for the book. I am pretty badly split up and concentration is slipping through my fingers. It is time for me to take a good short grip on myself and snub myself up tight to the hitching post. Well, I can do that. I can see mistakes with the boys but I wonder whether I could do better.

Now I will try to get back to the work. Samuel has now to meet Adam Trask and Lee for the last time. I want to make a fine thing of this. I will tell you now what I intend. I want Samuel to become a kind of a huge figure of folklore. For that reason I am not going to take the reader to his death. I have already described it early in the book. I will only report it in this part. In this way I will keep him partly alive like a frog's heart in saline solution or like the memory of a man.

Now I have talked to you on the phone and it doesn't seem so far away. There are advantages to a telephone after all. I'm sorry it is hot there. It is so fine here. But then, your office is cool. It is when you have to leave it that hurts.

Now the week and the week's rhythm. It would be so much better if I didn't ever stop but I don't have enough energy for that. The new pages pile up in typescript. It is getting to be a thick book at least on typing paper. Wouldn't it be fine if I didn't miss much time this summer? I would have a great section of E of E finished. You are right—the title seems to stick. I think of it pretty much by that handle now and it seems right. I will get a card off to you today. I keep thinking I have written to you when all I have done is fill in these working notes. You must admit they are very full and I imagine much of them very dull.

Now I read that the Russians have suggested a cease fire.* If we haven't figured their policy yet, I think we are crazy. They press until the pressure from us equalizes and then they give and start it in another area. It seems to me that when they press we should press in some area of their weakness as well as meeting their pressure. We seem to do almost exactly what they want us to do. I'm going to get into this thing pretty soon. I have lots of ideas. And now I will get back to my knitting.

June 26, Tuesday

It is now four months since I have been on this book. And it seems to go a little over a hundred pages a month. That is pretty good as an average. I would not be ashamed of that. It would make me about half way through the novel now but I really don't know. Yesterday I didn't get as far along in the story as I had

---

* In Korea.

thought because I had to put in the cosmogony of Eliza. She was no lay figure in the family but a pillar of great strength. And I had to say how and of what it consisted. Then I got Samuel to the Trask place. Now it seems to me that Adam Trask has faded. I want him to fade but not to die. In other words, before I finish this next scene, I want to give the reader some glimpse into the world he has retired to. Now it is my opinion that many people thwarted build their desired life behind their eyes and live in it. I think that Adam never really gave Cathy up. I think he is living with the Cathy he invented. And I wonder how I am going to get that over in the book. I think I know. It is fascinating how method assembles itself. The man who holds on to an impossibility is a frightening spectacle to many people and yet that is exactly what we all do more or less. It is simply a matter of degree.

Now—I presume the manuscript arrived yesterday. I think you would be burning up the wires by now if it had not. And there is no reason why it should not. I shall try to get it in the mail every Friday afternoon, which means it will go out by air Saturday at eleven and be delivered Monday in the first delivery. And I am requesting a reply card every time to be sure you get it. I shall be glad to know what you think of last week's work. This is a great section on Hamilton—the last great section save only one. There will be a Trask section, then the final one on Tom and that will be the last important contribution of the Hamiltons except for small sections. My patterned book is clear to me now —right to the end. And I am pleased that I am able to follow the form I laid down so long ago. I hope the book will sound a little formless at first until it settles in the mind. One thing interests me and in a way frightens me. I am deeply immersed in the book and so are you. I wonder if it is interesting—to anyone else, I mean. I hope you gave Elizabeth the rest of it. I want her icy opinion. It has never failed me. I just don't know whether my devilish playing with the verities will be interesting in a time when speed and action are the only literary interests. If my book should be liked, it will mean that at last there is a revulsion for the immediate and a slight desire to return to the contemplative. But we shall see. I know it is the best book I have ever done. I don't know whether it is good enough. You know better than anyone what this book means to me. Do you remember the struggle in the Bedford Hotel when I knew and did not know that Gwyn had rejected me? And all the notes and tries and false starts? Of course you do. It was franticness and then it was ready and it came normally, but do you know, Pat, I don't think it could have been done without all the preceding nonsense.

And I guess that is about all now. I will get to work.

June 26, *continued*

Well, there's today's work. And I hope you will like it. Is it too talky? Samuel has always been a talky man. Is it interesting? And did I get over his secret life well without ever having him say it?

Now tomorrow I will have a final statement of my theme and it will never again be mentioned in the book. With the death of Samuel the whole tempo of the book is going to change just as the tempo of the times changed. It will speed and rage then. You'll see. I manage to stay excited about this book. It has never been dull to me. I hope it will not be for other people. I feel both humble and proud about this book. It's an odd feeling. I've never felt quite so about anything of mine. I'm trying to write the microcosm. I have a little feeling that I am succeeding. Some of tomorrow's work is going to be very funny, I think. A really amusing venture in scholarship. But I must leave space for certain words which I have asked you to give me. I'll fill the word in later together with the definition you will find for me. And that is all for today and I am satisfied with today's work.

June 27, *Wednesday*

Very early to work. Always a problem. One with the boys right now. But we'll work it out. I think Pascal can help us to work it out. That's why I wanted his address. He has learned a great deal and I should like his help. I think I noted earlier in these pages that I had never done anything without having a problem. And this is no exception. But we're going to beat this one.

Now to thoughts of work. It is raining today, by the way, and the boys cannot go outside. This makes for quite a lot of noise. Noise is bad only sometimes. At others one can work under a cement mixer and never hear it. I don't know how it is going to be today. We'll just have to see. I'm a little nervous because of last night's crisis but not too badly nervous. I can take care of nearly anything now. In the matter of the boys, I just wish I knew more. And there's where Pascal can help me. I keep getting back to that subject. It must be deeply on my mind. I think I will write Pascal today and enclose it in a note to you. That way he will get it quicker.

I know you must have got last week's mss. by now. This week's work is shaping up. Seems to be having the roundness I want it to have. If you will look over the meeting of Adam and Samuel in yesterday's work, you will find it packed with information both about the men and about the story. I think it was pretty good work. It was talky but it had to be I guess. There is no physical movement in memory. But it must be interesting. I will soon be wanting someone who knows nothing about it at all to be reading the whole thing. Jean Ainsworth read the first part and never spoke of it—not one word. I didn't ask her of course. But she is not communicative. She read From Here to Eternity in page proof and had only one comment—that it was too long. I haven't read it but I gather that this was good criticism. Now I want E of E to be long but not too long. And as you will notice, I am trying to get away from a feeling of length by constant change of pace. You went back and read all so far in one clump. Did you find it long? Before much time, I should like Pascal to read what is done so far. He will have a clear eye for flaws. I must have at least four hundred and fifty pages now. Do you remember how many mss. (typescript) pages there were in Grapes? I'm under the impression there were about 600 or 650. I now think this book will be 800 typescript pages. It may be slightly more or less.

Now, I think I indicated, but I will reiterate—after the death of Samuel, the whole tempo and tone of the story is going to change. It will speed and leap toward the future. And now I guess it is time to get to the work of today and I hope you will find it good.

June 28 [THURSDAY]

I am delighted that you are coming to the island even though it is a month off. And we will have fun. I should have another hundred pages done by then. But I will not take any time off for you. There is no need. I go to work about eight and it's a rare day when I am not finished by one. And since we will have no reason to roister at night I can continue that and we still will have a fine time. I think we are winning the battle of Tom but it will be very gradual. I am really quite worried about him.

He needs help and right now. Sometime I will tell you about the talk I had with him yesterday. I talked to him as though he were an adult or at least my equal and I think a lot more got through than you can imagine.

Last night I read the first three days of this week to Elaine and she says she likes it the best in the whole book. Certainly I do not think that the Cain-Abel story has ever been subjected to such scrutiny. Nor has any story been so fruitful of meaning. Today, I am filled with lassitude. I wanted Lee's statement of faith to be so simple and so beautiful that there could be no doubt of its truth. I know it needs polishing but I think the thought is down. And I am a little drained. But that's all right. One is never drained by work but only by idleness. Lack of work is the most enervating thing in the world.

There needs today to be the end of the kind of music which is Samuel Hamilton. It has to have first a kind of recapitulation with full orchestra, and then I would like a little melody with one flute which starts as a memory and then extends into something quite new and wonderful as though the life which is finishing is going on into some wonderful future. I want Samuel to go out with wonder and interest. This man must not be defeated even though he may feel defeat all around him. It is the fashion now in writing to have every man defeated and destroyed. And I do not believe all men are destroyed. I can name a dozen who were not and they are the ones the world lives by. It is true of the spirit as it is of battles—the defeated are forgotten, only the winners come themselves into the race. And Samuel I am going to try to make into one of those pillars of fire by whom little and frightened men are guided through the darkness. The writers of today, even I, have a tendency to celebrate the destruction of the spirit and god knows it is destroyed often enough. But the beacon thing is that sometimes it is not. And I think I can take time right now to say that. There will be great sneers from the neurosis belt of the south, from the hard-boiled writers, but I believe that the great ones, Plato, Lao Tze, ~~Bhduh~~ how the hell do you spell Bhudda, Christ, Paul, and the great Hebrew prophets are not remembered for negation or denial. Not that it is necessary to be remembered but there is one purpose in writing that I can see, beyond simply doing it interestingly. It is the duty of the writer to lift up, to extend, to encourage. If the written word has contributed anything at all to our developing species and our half developed culture, it is this: Great writing has been a staff to lean on, a mother to consult, a wisdom to pick up stumbling folly, a strength in weakness and a courage to support sick cowardice. And how any negative or despairing approach can pretend to be literature I do not know. It is true that we are weak and sick and ugly and quarrelsome but if that is all we ever were, we would millenniums ago have disappeared from the face of the earth, and a few remnants of fossilized jaw bones, a few teeth in strata of limestone would be the only mark our species would have left on the earth. Now this I must say and say right here and so sharply and so memorably that it will not be forgotten in the rather terrible and disheartening things which are to come in this book; so that although East of Eden is not Eden, it is not insuperably far away.

Does this chapter* seem to go on too long? There are so many things I want to say in it. And so at the risk of being over-long, I am going to carry it through and finish this chapter perhaps tomorrow. But maybe not. But I am sure I will finish it tomorrow because I want to send it to you in one piece. I want you to feel it or reject it as a whole. It is necessary to my book because my book is about everything. What you had today was the full orchestra I spoke of. Now tomorrow I will take up the little flute melody, the continuing thing that bridges lives and ties the whole thing together, and I will end with a huge chord if I can do it. I know how I want it to sound and I know how I want it to feel and I know how I want you to feel when you have read it. And do you know I think as I go on that this is the only affirmation in writing in a very long time. And now I am going out in the boat to fish and to think about my melody. And I will put my melody in the mail for you tomorrow.

June 29 [FRIDAY]

Your letter came yesterday and I am very glad you like last week's work. I am coming now to the end of another week's work and I don't know whether I will finish today or not. If not I will finish tomorrow and you should get it Monday. Today's work is very difficult. You will have noticed that my flute passage of yes-terday took a sharp and terrible new melody—that Samuel did something new and surprising, something you didn't expect he would do. Now, today perhaps you will see why. And today there must be affirmative statement. And I don't know whether I have

---

* Chapters 23 and 24.

the strength to do it all today. I'm a touch run down. Elaine and I stayed up reading and talking and arguing until five this morning. Great excitement in discussion. But the result is that we are a little tired today and I don't know whether I have the energy to finish the chapter. However, I will try. Yesterday was very cold and windy. We were going fishing but decided not to because the wind was icy and the waters can be dangerous in this weather. Today is sunny and we may go late this afternoon. I feel very willy-nilly today. Isn't that strange. I have never been more excited in my life about a chapter than I have been in this one which is just now concluding. I must say that. In the doing, that is. I haven't gone back over it. I know it needs lots of work but the form and the content of it seem right to me and right for the design of the book. I have the same reluctance you have to lose Samuel except that we won't lose him. That is one of the theses that I tried to put in my book of notes yesterday and some of which I am going to try to transpose into my story, either now or later. I need power today. I need very quiet but very strong power. And I'd better get to some of it now.

Later. Well that's the end of the chapter and I will send it this afternoon. And I hope you like it.

July 2, Monday

Now, how did it get to be this time of the year. The last time I looked up it was March. And in other ways I seem to have been writing on this book forever. I guess the last is true. I have been writing on this book all of my life. And throughout, you will find things that remind you of earlier work. That earlier work was practice for this, I am sure. And that is why I want this book to be good, because it is the first book. The rest was practice. I want it to be all forms, all methods, all approaches.

When I finished last week's work, I thought it was the end of the era. But there is one thing more. And it must come today. Maybe it will be longer because it is very important. And when I finish it, there will be definitely the end of Part II.* That generation will be done. And it will be time for the second or rather the third generation. And I think I will have a cleaner start at it if only I make the next Part III. This means that there will be four parts to this book instead of three. And that is perfectly all right

---

* Now in Part Three.

with me. I am not going to put artificial structures on this book. The real structures are enough, I mean the discipline imposed by realities and certain universal writers. Oh Lord I hope it is good. Maybe you won't like the piece I am going to do today. It must go in, however. It really must. There will be some revelations in it that will explain other things. Anyway it is going down.

This morning is the most beautiful sunny, clear morning. But the clouds are beginning to drift in and maybe the whole day will not be this way. The boys are better this week. Maybe they are leaping over the transition time. They do seem better to me. Maybe I am better, too. I hope I am.

I am going through pencils at a great rate. The damp air here seems to make the leads softer although that hardly seems possible. Anyway, I only have three dozen out of the six dozen you got me. So I guess you had better be prepared to buy me another six dozen. I had thought that this six dozen would finish the book but it will probably take another 12 dozen. This is one hell of a long book.

Now I had better get into today's work. It is full of strange and secret things, things which should strike deep into the unconscious like those experimental stories I wrote so long ago. Those too were preparation for this book and I am using the lessons I've learned in all the other writing.

I will be so anxious to know Harold's reaction to the book thus far. Do please let me know what it is as soon as you can. I am wondering what effect its slow and roving method will have on him. It might leave him absolutely cold. This book is either going to have a great impact or none at all. I don't think there will be anything in between. And now to the work.

July 3, Tuesday

It is a most beautiful day. Elaine has taken the boys on a picnic leaving me with a long day to work. It is the loveliest of days, bright sun but cool and beautiful. And I look forward to time. And today I am going to need it. I suppose I am becoming a monomaniac about the book. Everything takes place about it from the blackest of magic to the purest of science. Maybe silly. I think of things like this: East of Eden is dominated by E's. Elaine is sometimes called E and so signs her name. Therefore the letter is lucky. I think of the book as E.

Last night I hardly slept at all. It was one of those good

thinking nights. Until 12 I carved a paddle for Tom to use on his rubber boat. Then to bed to think all night. Over the week end I realized a great lack in this book. It is to fill that lack that this chapter which yesterday I called an envoi is designed. But it turns out to be much more than an envoi. It turns out to be one of the most important chapters in the book (I almost said boat). And it was about that I was thinking all night. When you read this chapter you will realize how catastrophic it would have been to have left it out. One whole note or melody would not be there. Isn't it strange? And I think I have worked it out, as you will see in today's work. But again it is one of those growing chapters and I am by no means sure that I can finish it today. It must be superbly well done and I want to take plenty of time with it. Here two forces meet and for the first time the good force wins a temporary victory. But it is real warfare.

Tomorrow is the 4th of July. I do not see any reason to take it off. I would take any personal holiday but it is nonsense to me to take public ones. In the first place I want to stay off the roads. The tourists are beginning to come in. But one thing is true. Not a great increase of cars so the highways are not cluttered, nor is Siasconset, but Nantucket will be a complete madhouse. I will stay at home and work. And maybe finish this chapter if I do not today. I am nervous about today's work. I get up and do other things which seem to need to be done. And I have just cut the finger that holds the pencil, not badly but enough so it is clumsy. This is usually a proof of a fear of work. And I don't know why it is because I think I am well prepared for this chapter. And maybe if I stop talking about it and just start it, it will be all right. I'll try that and now.

July 4, Wednesday

And I have a desire not to work today which I must not indulge. I don't know why this ferocious discipline but it seems good to me. I repaired my cut finger with nail polish to protect it from the pencil and it is just drying now. That's why the handwriting is strange. A bandage feels strange but clear nail polish is a fine covering.

Couldn't find any fireworks, not even sparklers. Next year I am going to have a cannon even if I have to make one. I don't know what to make of your letter with the Hebrew word. I'll have to know much more about the word than that. Maybe when you read the chapter, you will know more about what I want to know. May is a curious word in English. In the negative it is an order but in the positive it allows a choice. Thou mayest not is definite but thou mayest implies either way—do you see? But I can fill that in any time and I will have to be sure of my etymology before I do because such a passage will invite the closest scrutiny. Also I will be glad to know what you think of the passage. If the book is read, it will start great arguments and the best scholarship will be brought to bear.

The work today is very tense. In fact I do not know whether I can get the quality in it I want. It scares me a little. I guess I should plow right into it but I am not quite ready yet. I don't know why.

I had a good letter from Pascal which I will answer some time this week. But it will require thought and my thinking is pretty much taken up this week with my book. But I might as well get to it.

Now it is done. And maybe tomorrow I will finish the chapter and maybe not. Because I feel that it is important to my theme, I am going to let it take as long as it wants. Also I need it for another maturation for the future. So don't worry about its length. It is going to be all right.

And now I shall celebrate the 4th of July without even a sparkler. We are not drinking anything but beer. I'm going to have a can right now.

So there!!

July 5, Thursday

Although not a humanitarian, I do have certain human kindnesses and it does seem to me that these notes may be boring the hell out of you. So I will give you an antidote. There is no need for you to read them. You will never be questioned and it is unlikely that anyone will ever know. I hope this reassures you and makes it less a burden to you.

You would be interested in my fingers, I think. I have designed pieces of rubber bandage to protect them from the pencil. They are so beat up that they hurt but my new method works fine.

In the evening I am doing a little wood carving while listening to bad radio music. I have tried to read but I find I don't pay any attention to the script of the book because I am always thinking of my own. A real monomaniac.

The Bartlett arrived this morning. Isn't it funny that I have always wanted one and needed one and never had one? I would like you to buy me another one to give as a present. Would you do that? And do all these requests and commissions bother you? You have only to say and I will stop it. Don't let me impose on you. I don't mean to but maybe I go too far. I do depend on you for so much.

Now back to E. This scene is developing and I am interested in its tensions and I hope I am making clear what is happening in both people. It may seem a strange or outlandish situation but, with perhaps less violence, it is what happens all the time between people. And I think people might find some of it in themselves. And now I guess I have put enough down here. And I will get to my knitting. I don't think I will finish the scene today, however. It is a very important scene, not only now, but for later.

July 6 [FRIDAY]

It hardly seems possible that this could be the end of the third working week since I have been here. But the pages say that it is. I'm glad you like last week's work. I don't think you will *like* this week's. It isn't likeable but I think it might be effective. And I know now that it is necessary.

Yesterday we had Dorothy's nice letter. Elaine is going to write her about clothes. I think we are working Tom over. He has made remarkable progress. [. . .] He is excited about working and we just have to keep it up. Elaine is doing wonders with him. There will be other outbreaks but we are equipped to deal with them now.

I feel just worthless today. I have to drive myself. I have used every physical excuse not to work except fake illness. I have dawdled, gone to the toilet innumerable times, had many glasses of water. Really childish. I know that one of the reasons is that I dread the next scene, dread it like hell. You will know why when you read it because there isn't any doubt that I will get it done today. I do not often permit myself to get away with nonsense. And I want this scene finished. Then I will have the week end to prepare Part 3 and its opening. And I will need the two days for it. But right now I am giving myself trouble like a stubborn kid.

I was very glad of your last letter. And the translation of the word. Don't worry about it. I will have to get the best answers. And if there is an argument I am all right. Don't forget that in the Jewish translation you sent, they did not think "timshel" was a pure future tense. They translated it "thou mayest." This means that at least there is a difference of opinion and that is enough for me. I will have to have the whole verb before I will finish, from infinitive on through past, subjunctives and compounds and futures. But we will get it. We may have to go outside of rabbinical thought to pure scholarship which may be non-Jewish. What American university has a good Hebrew department? Dr. Ginzberg,* dealing in theology, may have a slightly different attitude from that of a pure etymologist. We know that the other translations were warped by what the translators wished to be there. Words are strange elusive things and no man may permanently stick them on pins or mount them in glass cases. The academies have tried that and have only succeeded in killing the words. But why I should lecture you I don't know.

I'm going to rap my knuckles with a stick and force it now and we will see. This chapter must be mailed by tomorrow noon —must.

There—that damnable chapter † is finished. But I think you can see why it was necessary. Maybe you understand Cathy a little better. And now Adam is ready to go into Part 3. And so am I. But I wouldn't have been unless I had done this last chapter.

You won't like this chapter but you will understand it. Now the balance is achieved and we know where everybody stands.

And so farewell.

July 9, Monday

This is a milestone day. The start of a new Part of the book. And I have thought and thought until my head was swimming. I have the fear that comes with starting and the usual lack of self-confidence. But also there is a kind of craziness it is hard to peg down—a willy-nilly, fly-off-to-the-ends-of-the-world feeling. And I must pull this down to a normal living and a regularity of thinking. It would be easy to say that I am tired. But I am not. I've been with book a long time now and I am not tired. And it is rare

---

* Covici had referred the question to Dr. Louis Ginzberg of the Jewish Theological Seminary.
† Chapter 25.

now for me to be frightened of it. This is temporary. What is it then that is bothering me? I don't know. It isn't the boys. They are making great strides. Tom has come around beautifully. I feel badly that I didn't know he would. Both boys are being just fine. They are responding beautifully.

Let me inspect then the book itself. It must be nearly 500 pages by now. It started by saying, "I'm going to tell you how things were then." Now, has it done that? I don't know. I just don't know. It left customs and clothes and habits and went deeply into people but I think that is very good rather than bad. For customs are only the frame for people. You can't write a book about customs unless it is a treatise. And I don't want a treatise. I want the participation of my reader. I want him to be so involved that it will be *his* story. You are tied up in this story very deeply. I doubt whether you can see what has been accomplished because, through these notes, you know what the intention is. And perhaps because you know what was intended, you may believe that it has been accomplished. To that extent, these notes may be bad. I don't know.

Today, the work is bound to be slow. All week end I thought about it. The new section is about to start. It is a change in time, a change in direction. The nation, the Valley are changing their direction and also their tempo. How am I going to indicate this? I don't know. I want to keep the curious relaxed feeling. Maybe the best way will be simply to tell the truth about it. Maybe the hardest thing in writing is simply to tell the truth about things as we see them. That might be so. I have surely tried to do that in this book. I would hate to lose it in literary trickery now.

You know from the form feeling in your stomach that I am more than half way finished now. Not that the book is drawing to its close, but it is all down now. Its thesis is stated—all of it. Now we will see the thesis at work. Do you feel that? I hope so. I don't want you, and by you I mean the reader, to be conscious of the thesis. That should sink deeply under the skin and only the people be remembered and thought about.

This is an old mess of a day. I don't care whether I get my two pages done, but I probably will. I usually do. But I want to be inspective about it too. There has not been a book like this that I know of. Its leisure derives from 18th-century English novels, but it goes from that to the intense. The 18th-century novel projected people and ideas but they were set apart from the reader for his inspection. This attempts to use both, the old and the new. I don't know whether or not it succeeds. That is why I want to hear Harold's reaction. I am not writing you off but you are in effect one of the writers and have lost your separate standing. You will have difficulty being a critic I think although I may be wrong. I am going to continue these notes and today I do not feel that it is either dawdling nor putting it off. And I want to ask you some questions that I wouldn't have put in last week's notes. Were you conscious of what happened to Adam in the last chapter? I have repeated that good things do not die. Did you feel that Samuel had got into Adam and would live in him? Did you feel the rebirth in him? Should I make it clearer or were you aware of it? Men do change, do learn, do grow. That is what I want to get into that last. And also, do you understand Cathy better now? You should, if I have done my work right. Her life is one of revenge on other people because of a vague feeling of her own lack. A man born blind must in a sense hate eyes as well as envy them. A blind man might wish to remove all of the eyes in the world. That last is a terrible chapter and maybe the best writing about people I have ever done in my life.

I am nearly ready to start Part 3 now. I am going back to Part 1 for my tempo. Refrain is one of the most valuable of all form methods. Refrain is return to the known before one flies again upwards. It is a consolation to the reader, a reassurance that the book has not left his understanding.

To a certain extent I have thought about the reception of this book. And it seems to me that it might find a public ready for the open and honest. As you know the novel has been falling before the onslaught of non-fiction. That is largely because the novel has not changed for a very long time now. Sherwood Anderson made the modern novel and it has not gone much beyond him. I think I am going beyond him. This may be rejected and kicked down but I do not think so. I really don't. However, this is a conjecture which will be demonstrated.

One thing I must say—I have never enjoyed my own work as I have this book. I am as excited about it now as on the day I started it. There is no letdown in my energy. I still think it is The Book, as far as I am concerned. Always before I have held something back for later. Nothing is held back here. This is not practice for a future. This is what I have practiced for. I do not know what I will do when it is finished. I will have some difficulty in living. I think there will be a bad time but I'll weather that when

I come to it. The book is a thing in itself, and it is not *me*. There is no ego in it. I am glad that you sense that while I am in it and of it, I am not the book. It is much more than I am. The pictures have come to me out of some hugeness and sometimes they have startled me. But I am glad of them.

Now I am ready to shove off again and as the Catholics say, I will be glad to be remembered in your prayers.

July 10, Tuesday

Yesterday's work was hard and at the same time rewarding. I think I accomplished what I wanted to do. It must go on in the economic change today. What, by the way, do you think of the analysis of the change? I happen to think it is true. As happens so often after a difficult day, no sleep last night but that doesn't beat me a bit. It just means that I got a great deal of future work laid out. And the loss of one night doesn't even seem to tire me. Which is a good thing. I start today a little tense but fresh. Elaine is taking the boys into Nantucket for haircuts. They are going to have dinner guests.

The little present you gave me is in use every day. With it I can do almost anything. I have carved many things and there are pin wheels all over the place. I am even carving you a present which is a form I have never used before. And I hope you will like it. So far it is much the best thing I have carved. And rather good if I do say so myself. Now I have lots of time.

Perhaps because of the tenseness of the scene, I got pretty wound up last week. And I was scared of the new section also, but now I am not and I can get back that fine relaxed feeling I have had for this book for so long. Surely though it is necessary that I more or less live in the tempo of what I am writing. That must be inevitable.

There is one other thing about this book different from any I have ever done. Of course I am doing the best work I can but I am not taking myself too seriously. This is no assault on Parnassus. I am not putting grappling hooks into immortality. It is just a book—the best I can do with the equipment and training I have. And I'm pretty sure if I knew no one in the world would ever read it, I would still do it. I wonder whether that last is true. It seems so to me but being sure what one would do in a situation one hasn't experienced is rather silly. And if it is true, why am I so anxious to know what you are getting out of it and whether you approve or disapprove. Still—I think I would write it anyway.

Juan Negrin is coming up in the middle of August for a week end. He is such a good friend. I use his skill and his kindness all the time and I am unable to return anything. And his eyes looked very tired to me. I talked to him on the phone and he said he was pleased with your progress but doesn't want you to stop the medication. I am going to ask him perhaps for a present and it has been considered the greatest gift of all. He is a good man, Pat. He has savagery and violence and courage. He is not afraid to take a chance in surgery. He would take a life to gain a life. And I like that kind of courage. I have thought too how a surgeon, particularly a brain surgeon, is very much alone in his decisions. He can't ask for advice, for who is to give? It must take the greatest moral courage and a kindness that is far beyond softness or gentleness. He must in a word be part child, part savage and part god. And with that I will get back to my book which is more child and savage than God and that is a very good thing.

July 11, Wednesday

Last night an evil came on me. I planned, laughing behind my hand, to play hooky today and go fishing and pick up my work on Saturday. My course was set and my criminal path taken. And then this morning was an overcast and windy sky. The very forces of nature conspired to keep me pure. But being pressured into virtue, I am having a very hard time getting started today. I wish I had been allowed to be the sinner I wanted to be. Maybe I need some sin.

I had fun with the economic section yesterday. Very few people ever reduce our system to its essential nonsense. And it should be done now and then if only to reassure ourselves that we are fools. I feel particularly a fool today. Sort of messy in the mind. I think I need a little rest and I know I would be very unhappy if I took one unless there were something like fishing to take up the strain. My fingers are not sore any more but they are really calloused. The cut on the tip of my fingers is hard as a rock. And I am unshaven. I don't shave every day here, not by any means. We heat our water with a little coal stove and that means we have to build a little fire to have a bath. So we don't bathe as often as we do at home but that doesn't make much difference since we are in the ocean so often, a thing which does not get us very clean but at least we don't smell bad.

Now it is late and I still haven't done anything. This is nothing but laziness—nothing. I am not stuck in my story. Do you remember once in New York I suddenly decided I was not going to work and didn't? I felt very good about that. Maybe it would be good for me to do it again. I'll have to think about that. And it might be good for you not to expect 10 pages every Monday. Maybe the regularity is hurting both of us. What do you think? I will have to think about that.

Well, I can't see any reason to sit here and shadow box. I ought either to go out and do other things or go to work. I think I will try both.

Well I did it anyway and it has taken all day. The day has been saddened by Tom's going on a tangent. It's almost like a sickness. I could feel it coming on this morning and it built and built through all of his symptoms to straight disobedience and now he is in coventry and that is hard on the whole house but it is the only thing that seems to get through to him. It can probably be removed by tomorrow morning but it might have to go on all day tomorrow too.

Now back to the book. I am through now with the introduction to Part 3 and ready to get back to my story.

And now I am knocking off.

July 13, Friday

Yesterday I took the day off and went fishing all day. I caught nothing but had a fine day on the water and got so burned that I am in considerable pain today. And had a rough night last night. It was so cool that I didn't know how I was burning. So I have a good reason not to work hard but not a good enough reason. I shall send the mss. at the usual time but it will only be four days, not five as usual. But since I intend to work tomorrow, there will probably be six days in the next batch. The sunburn pain will all be gone by tomorrow due to the glories of tannic acid which cuts it down quickly.

Now to E. The entrance into Part 3 is done and I am ready to get back to the story. And I am going back now to the method used in the very first of the book—the long-range narrative with small interspersed scenes to cover a transition in time. I feel all right about it. And I think it will be all right.

Your letter says among other things that Harold is bewildered at the mss. I hope you don't mean confused. It occurs to me that one might well be confused by the very weight of this god dammed book. You and I have had it day by day but if it landed in one's lap suddenly, it might have too great weight and complication. But such things we will see gradually. A book is as complicated as a life, in some ways more complicated. Right now I am so deeply immersed in E that I have a difficulty thinking outside of it. And I wonder in some ways what is going to happen. I mean I know the directions it is going to take but I don't know exactly the incidents.

In this I have always tried to tell you in advance what I am trying to do and I think that is a good thing, perhaps better for me than for you because it sets down the intention and purpose in advance and keeps the book from wandering. Very well, always going back to my C-A theme, the next section is going to reverse the first section. I will tell you what I mean. Do you remember in the first part the burden was with Adam who was the Abel? Even though it did not seem to, the book was seen through his eyes and through his emotions. Charles was a dark principle who remained dark. Think back and you will see that this is so. Now in Part 3 I am going to try to do just the opposite. Caleb is my Cain principle. I am going to put the burden of experience through his eyes and his emotions. And in the end you should know him pretty well. And since every man has Cain in him, he will be fully well understood. Part 3 is Caleb's part—since he dominates and survives it. Thus we get no repetition but an extension of Part 1. Now there is the plan and as the man says—let's see if you can do it. I feel free about it and good because I think in myself I have access to both Cain and Abel. There is the plan anyway and I am going to try it and I leave you to wonder how I am going to do it. I wonder myself.

Later. Now there is the end of my week's work as far as you are concerned. But I will work tomorrow because the story is going to quicken now and I want to get into it.

So long.

July 14, Saturday

Because I took Thursday off I am going to do some work today to make up for it. This is good for a number of reasons. First, it is good self-discipline, and second, if I do it, I will feel free some time in the middle of the week to take a day off and pick it up later. But I can only do this if I can prove to myself that I can do it. I have a kind of weariness from living three lives at once and now and then I get a little confused trying to keep them separate. And believe me this takes some doing. I wish I felt better today. And I do in everything but my mind and that is a little sick today. It is probably one of those curious cycles which in the female results in menstruation and in the male causes those depths of depression bordering on the maniac. It is probable that both have a rhythm printed some time on the species by some great impressive force of nature. But the fact that such a force is withdrawn does not make it any less. Maybe I will come out of it. Surely such a feeling changes the world around one.

I am purposely avoiding more discussion of the word "timshel" until I see you and talk to you. Your last letter which suggests "thou canst" moves even closer to free will than "thou mayest." And if there is still difference of opinions among scholars, my point is made.

The day started dark and sullen and only gradually is the sun creeping through. And it may not be a dour day after all. I suppose it would be a good thing for me if I did not dawdle any more but went right to work.

I had a letter from Harold, saying that he was going to be able to finish the mss. as so far typed this week end and he would report on it Monday. I gather from you that he has already read a good part of it.

I do hope the clouds begin to drift away from my mind. I'll add a note at the end of this to tell you whether or not they have.

Well there's the day's work. I had to do this scene because Lee is important. And do you know what is going to happen now? I'll bet you don't. I'll bet anything you don't.

And now, my sunburn permitting, I think I may go down to the beach and practice casting a little. That's good fun.

July 16, Monday

Another week out of the deck. This year the weeks are padding along like ducks in line. And this one will be gone quicker than most. Saturday night Elaine and I sat up sedately drinking gin and tonic. And she read me some parts of E because I had never heard it except in my own voice and I was amazed at the charge of emotion in it. I hadn't realized it carried so much but maybe that is only to us. Wouldn't you think that on Saturday night I could get away from the book? But I couldn't.

Today is going to be slow but I can't help it. Mondays are usually slow. But today I have a couple of new characters to develop. You have seen them before but I don't think you have known them. Now I must make you know them. It is hard to open up a person and to look inside. There is even a touch of decent reluctance about privacy but writers and detectives cannot permit the luxury of privacy. In this book I have opened lots of people and some of them are going to be a little bit angry. But I can't help that. Right now I can't think of any work which requires concentration for so long a time as a big novel.

I judge from the number of pages sent back now, 457 I think, that I must be well over five hundred by now. And I have little fear now, barring accidents, that I will have this book done and corrected and ready by Christmas. I have still my month of leeway I gave myself and I think I have used only three days of it. Two to move and one in New York when I just didn't work. I've caught up the fishing day last week.

I should now go to work because you must begin to know the twins and you must know them very very well because the next part of the book is going to be about them and one of them at least is going to dominate the last part of the book. It is my opinion that you should feel these twins and I am about to go to work on them. And naturally I am a little frightened at the assignment.

Now there is the day's work and I wonder whether in this little bit the qualities of the two boys begin to stick through. This is going to be the most careful development of character maybe of the whole book.

I am losing track of time. The weeks roll on and I am riding on their backs. In a very short time you will be here for a while and I must say I am looking forward to that time. I have much to talk about to you. Eden moves along. Last night E and I went over it generally to see whether it is fulfilling its purpose and staying within the banks of its design. And it is. Amazingly enough it has openness and it has not gone out of the path I set for it. I do not see how I have managed to do this but I have. Maybe the millions of words were not in vain after all. I like to think that anyway.

A great and beautiful storm today—such lightning and rain—and this always stimulates me like a drug. I must have great violence in me because I react to violence in nature with great joy. And a good thunder roll makes me feel almost as though I could do it myself. Today it is not so good because it makes me hesitate in going to work because I might miss something. Very well, I'll write it in. It is about time for something like that. And it is also about time for gaiety. The death of Samuel has removed gaiety from the world. And I have to put some back in. For Eden must be everything, not only the grim and terrible because that isn't the way life is. Life is silly too sometimes and that must be in it. Everything I have seen or heard or thought must go in and I feel the necessity for release now. Maybe to rest my audience for the next thing that has to happen.

My pencils are all short now and I think I will celebrate by getting out twelve new pencils. Sometimes the just pure luxury of long beautiful pencils charges me with energy and invention. We shall see. It means I will have to have more pencils before long though. Would you send me another box. They are Mongol 480 #2¾F round.

Well, here they are and I just sharpened them and oh! lord, I think my pencil sharpener is burning up. And if it is I'll be sick. I would have to have another one or have this repaired. When my work is done I will open it and see what is wrong. And if I can't correct it, you are likely to get a long-distance call and a hurry up. However, I may be able to find what is wrong. It just suddenly began to smoke and throw sparks. And it should not go out like this. I deeply depend on it. And now to work.

July 18, Wednesday

Well it took me the rest of the afternoon to fix the motor of the pencil sharpener and lots of thought. I found one of the carbons split and had to improvise pretty much, but I did it and this is remarkable because I don't know much about such things and I had to learn.

I hate to admit it, but a little weariness is creeping over me. I argue to myself that it is not so but it is. I think this. You are coming in a week and a half. I think I will plan to take a couple of days off to recuperate and to get some kind of change of pace. I know it is more than probable that I will not do this but it is nice to contemplate and restful to think about anyway.

Your notes on other versions of "thou canst" came yesterday and I can see that you, even as I am, are like a hound on the scent. And isn't it interesting that this word has been a matter of such concern for so long. You are having fun, aren't you? This is a time of great joy. It will never be so good again—never. A book finished, published, read—is always an anticlimax to me. The joy comes in the words going down and the rhythms crowding in the chest and pulsing to get out.

July 18 [19], Thursday

Very few notes today. Elizabeth Otis is coming this afternoon if the fog permits. She comes at 4 P.M. and I want to go to town and get some tools before that. So I am going to try to get done early with my work. It's a big day and the boys are wildly excited. They are picking flowers for Elizabeth's room. Tom has made her some paintings which he says she can take home and they are the best he has ever done.

Very fortunately I sat up very late last night at my wood carving and while I was at it, I worked out today's writing in detail. So it should not take very long.

Letter from Harold yesterday. He has reservations but very wisely doesn't tell me what they are now. On the whole he seems to like Eden. And it would be a startling thing to read for the first time.

A busy morning. The fuses just blew out. Well that's the way work must be done. Now let's see whether I can do it—right now.

July 20, Friday

This is a very unlikely day. It is going to be hard I think, very hard. Elizabeth's plane was very late last night, and we sat up late. I am going to make a real good try today and see if I can do it. I should like to get to page 50 today. That is fifty pages since we have moved. And that is pretty good I think. I haven't heard from you this week, I think because the planes have not been able to get in. For two days we were isolated by air with storms. That's what delayed Elizabeth.

Now, to Eden or at least a little East. Yesterday the children's scene, and I want to continue with it for a time today. I think I am making people of these children and this I must do. They must be real people. And this means that every word in every line of speech must be accurate and full of some kind of meaning which stretches not only forward in the book but stems from before in the book. And now, if I am going to do it, I think I had better get to it quickly. We shall see.

There it is, Pat, 50 pages since I have been here. Today was hard, very hard close work. And I hope you like it. Monday begins a new chapter.

And now I'll get this ready to go.

July 23, Monday

Elizabeth came on Thursday. I worked Friday as usual. And Friday night read her the week's work concerning the children which she and Elaine both liked. And I hope you will too. Next week end I will keep this mss. here because you will be here and perhaps I will read it to you. I have a nervousness today. Must have been very tired. Saturday night and last night I slept as though I had been drugged—long and deeply. Don't know why because I have been sleeping little and lightly. I have no consistencies. I guess that is it. All violences. Elaine is very steady and it only makes my lack of consistency and evenness more apparent. And it is not enough to say or to persuade myself that out of my nature I can do work. How much better might I not do it if I did have some kind of even keel. I don't have much introspection any more. Sometimes I observe tendencies with a certain alarm but I probe no more. Now that is enough of the personal. I am going to write you a letter at the end of the day embodying some of the silliest reasoning and thinking in the world. I am really very immature in many ways, perhaps in all ways.

Now back to the book—as always. In general, I am something more than half finished with it. I figure I have somewhere near 135,000 words done. I think another 100,000 will finish it. In fact I am pretty sure of it. And I don't even know how I know this except that I do. I think it is moving well now. One thing ends and another takes it up. I think the story keeps movement internally and externally but this is only my thought. I really don't know much about it. I have been so long at it that I don't know. Maybe I only hope it is going well. But that I surely do. Do you like Adam's awakening? Does he come out of it convincingly? He should. He is a living man again. And now things are about to happen—things which will make a change. And there is going to be a large change pretty soon. I'm sure you are aware of that. You must be. I have been planting the book full of the restlessness which precedes change. Just as history seems to ride up a series of plateaus, so does it seem to me that a man's life goes—up a little or down and then a flat place, and then another quick change and another plateau. In a book about a man, because of the restriction of space, the distance between the rises or falls is necessarily small and this must give a feeling of unreality. I am trying to overcome that by the use of techniques which indicate a longer time than that actual wordage would justify.

Now as you well know, Adam and his family must move down river toward the mouth. They will stop in Salinas for this generation. The last part will be at Moss Landing where the river enters the sea. This was the plan from the beginning and it is going to be followed so that my physical design remains intact and clear. Then it will be considered an accident. I don't know why writers are never given credit for knowing their craft. Years after I have finished a book, someone discovers my design and ascribes it either to a theft or an accident. And now I shall get back to my job.

July 24, Tuesday

If you are like me, you are getting very excited now about coming up here. I never lose the excitement. It strikes just as hard always. I am on the train or plane two or three days before it is due to start. This is hard on women because I am gone, in my mind at least, before they have begun to pack. How we are looking forward to your arrival. Today the wind shifted and started blowing in from Spain and I am told that means clear and lovely and warm weather.

I am late getting to work this morning. I got up early and I am kind of luxuriating in contemplation of my day's work. It is very funny. I sat with Elaine and told her the whole history of the Chinese in California as far as I knew it. And all of this as a background for the few paragraphs I am going to do today. Lord—if you put down all that went in back of a long book, it would be endless. And I must be careful not to overload this book—to keep the story straight and true when my impulse is to tell everything to this book. Well anyway, I tell nearly everything to these notes.

I am going to work on the present I am making for you while you are here. I think you might like to watch the process of trial and error. You don't love tools and working with your hands as much as I do but I think you like to watch it. So you shall and it will not interfere at all with conversation. Elaine asked whether you and Dorothy would want to go out to our few night clubs and I said that I was sure of few things but one of them is that you do *not* want to go to bars and night clubs. We have only been to one since we have been here and then for dinner.

I think while you are here I will try to go to work even earlier than I ordinarily do so that I can get through earlier.

And I think I will go to work now.

July 25, Wednesday

I sat up late last night, thinking and carving wood. I made a little whale, but from memory. Hadn't anything to model from. And maybe that's good. But I can't remember exactly how the flukes of a sperm whale go. Yesterday the story of Lee's parents ran over two pages so I finished it. Gave me one page up on the week. Today I have to write a letter, or at least have Adam write a letter, and I rather think that will be the day's work. Got your card yesterday. I had no intention of sending the manuscript this week. The weather is beautiful. I hope it stays that way.

Later. Well there's the letter Adam wrote and I have tried to fill it with the reticences a man would feel together with the revealing things that creep through.

July 26, Thursday

Not much in the way of notes today because you will be here tomorrow. Also I am late today, very late. I didn't sleep at all last night, planned work ahead and forgot the transition and have been all morning working it out. I know dialogue a month ahead and I didn't know this morning's transition. Also Catbird has a mild sunstroke, just enough to make him a little unhappy. And my neck aches from straining against work. And when I put the transition down that I have fought for all morning, it will sound so easy and so casual, I think. My nerves are a little jumpy. No sleep, I guess. I have very many things to talk to you about. Oh! very many and of course I will forget all of them. Tom is doing pictures for you, and I think very good ones. Everyone is preparing something and now I must really get to work. Or I won't get it done and if there is any not to be done I would rather it would be next week.

And now it is time.

July 27, Friday

Well today is the day you are coming. And I think you as I are probably up very early and generally in the way of that organism the "packing female." You may have women of every appearance and every temperament and every grade of intelligence but if you put a suitcase in front of them, they all become exactly alike. And have you noticed that when packing the female has a strong distaste for the male. She just doesn't want him around.

Well the notes next week will probably be pretty slim because we will have discussed everything in between but it will be fun and all a part of it.

The kids are riotous with excitement over your coming. And they have started so early that they probably will be cranky and mean by the time you get here. And now to the book.

I don't expect you to like the part I am on now as much as some people will. But to many men, it will strike a long burning bill of memory. You didn't grow up with the model-T Ford just a little higher than the end man of the trinity but many millions did.

July 30, Monday

The working notes are bound to suffer during the time you are here because I talk them out instead of writing them out. Today I am going to have trouble getting started. I think maybe I talked too much over the week end. I should never tell what is going to happen. It really hurts the writing. And I hope you will never ask any more. It's as though I let the story down to tell before I write it, at least in these notes.

I ate too much over the week end. Must go on starvation to get my hunger back. I just can't eat like that and keep any awareness. Food, too much of it, has a much worse effect on me than too much alcohol. I guess different bodies react differently. Overeating poisons not only my body but slugs my mind into insensibility. And I ate more in the last three days than is ordinary in a week for me. I'll gradually work it off and out, I guess. I'm having a hard time going to work because of it. My brain feels fat.

I've started the boys walking to town today. Gave them money for cones. I think it will be good for them to explore. City kids are so timid about getting lost. I want ours to learn to set out on their own.

I hope you are getting a good rest. You really need it. But you do have remarkable recuperative powers. I can almost see you snap back by the minute. And I'm glad for you to see the carving of the box to hold this manuscript. Now you will know how much goes into it. If I had finished it alone you would not have known the hours and hours that went into it. It's a good thing to see. And maybe you will get some small tools to work with. I think it is good for both hands and brain, and when you finish, you have made something and even if it isn't very good it is yours.

And now to work or to try to.

August 1, Wednesday

I didn't see you yesterday. Got into story trouble and when that happens, there's nothing to do but be alone and think. I didn't sleep at all last night but I think I got it ironed out and I am ready to go to work on it. Called you at the hotel but they said you were not down yet. It is a grey and rainy day. It matches my spirits which are wearied with thinking. And it is such a small matter which puzzled me. But to me it was insuperable. In today's work you will see how it is worked out and you probably won't be aware of my problem. It was subject and presentation of a curious moral thing. And it's a thing which is so delicate that probably a great many people would not know of its existence in the book. Anyway, thinking it out I did a hell of a lot of sand-papering. And now I am going to get to work. See how the notes diminish when you are here.

My sweet Elaine sat many hours with me last night while I put out a thundering silence. I can't bear anyone else around at such a time.

Later. And there you have it. And maybe you can see the complication and the reason I couldn't sleep last night.

August 2, [THURSDAY], *Tom's Birthday*

A beautiful crisp day with a suggestion of fall in the air. It's just a promise of frost and will not last long. But I love the little sharpness of it. So tired last night that I was nearly crazy. I toppled over into unconsciousness and this morning was all re-covered. And to wake up to this really lovely day. Tom got his presents, a boat and a watch and a knife, and he is very pleased. They are going to the pond to swim, if they make it.

I feel a little mixed up. Too many things happening I guess. I get confused. The single-track mind is overloaded. And the only danger is that I might turn mean. I almost always do when my pups of thought are endangered. You will probably regret that you came to the island because I am not very pleasant when I am working and sometimes I am downright nasty. I am not very large in that but I try.

A cousin of mine—Pat Hamilton, son of George, grandson of Samuel and the only bearer of the name, the only one (isn't that odd)—died two days ago. He was an incurable alcoholic and died of a heart attack after a two-weeks' drunk. And there lies that family name. I have the blood and my sons but he had the name. I feel badly that he did not wear it well. He left it no pride and surely no shine. In fact he dirtied it. The others though some of them were violent, at least were not sordid. This is the tragedy of a name. Well *hic jacet.*

Now because it is my son's birthday, I should get to work and have it done so I can play with him and do all the things that will make the day important. This is his most important day so far because with today he is a boy and he must renounce his babyhood. It is one of the hardest changes we make. And some never make it. But he will have to try, poor kid. We will help him and also we will insist on it. Tom has made great strides this year, particularly this summer. Now to work.

August 3, Friday

The birthday is over and I am nearly over. I have a very great weariness today. The weight of thinking seems too heavy to me. I guess I need a rest and I'm not going to get it. Complication and confusion—trying to do several things at once and they all fail. I find I am hurrying to get through my day's work. And that is going to stop. I'll lose any relaxed quality if it does. The other day you made a joke—I hope it was a joke—about increasing my word rate. That isn't even a joke. It is a destructive suggestion and not even to be joked about. A book, as you know, is a very delicate thing. If it is pressured, it will show that pressure. So—no more increases. My first impulse on such a suggestion is to stop entirely for a while and get my breath back. This is a really bad time in the book. I need time and lots of it. And I am going to get it too if people get hurt. It seems to require a certain meanness. And I have it. I'm really mixed up today. A book takes so long that people get tired waiting. I know that. But I said at the beginning that this had to be written as though it would never be done. And if I lose that feeling for any reason, the book will go to hell. So please let's remember that. After all this work I would rather put it away for a year than to spoil it now. This is all the result of weariness. I know that. But I can't help my weariness.

Now today I have a little interim thing that should be well done. And I don't know whether or not I can do it. In other words, it's a very hard day. Very hard. I don't know how to go about it. But it is time. And I'll have to do it.

August 6, Monday

Now you go on back to New York and I go back to my book. A real bad *crise de nerfs* last night caused by some kind of exhaustion or confusion or something, but a mad one of really ragged nerves. The long sleeps have been so full of dreams that they have little rest. Maybe like the Hamiltons I am over-engined for my chassis. I hope not. I want to finish this book. Beyond that I have not really thought much. But there is always the worry that I will not be able to finish it. And I don't know why such a thing occurs to me. Guess my resistance is low. That's all I can think of. And the threshold is low to irritations. This I am going to control. In fact the controls are going back on right now. The rawness doesn't very often show through, I hope.

Now I will go to my story and maybe get the pain out of my guts for a while in that. The episode is that of Dessie and Tom. And in effect it is a kind of a dreadful story. It is the end of the Hamiltons in one sense and in one direction. In all of it you will find a kind of play-acting, like children being kings and queens. That has always seemed very sad to me and how much sadder if it is grown-up people playing at kings and queens. That's what this is—a travesty. And I have to put it in. For a while I thought I could leave it out, but I guess I can't. From the first it has been integrated in my mind with the story, the whole story. I wonder whether it is going as I had intended. We find these crises very often. And there is one other thing. Our family always thought that Dessie went back to the ranch to take care of Tom. But her love was gone and no one ever thought that she might have gone back in search of her father, or the safety, or the warmth she needed. Of all her family Tom was most like her father and it was the seat she ran to. Maybe she was only running back to her childhood. I don't know but it seems reasonable. And I think that's the way I will have to see it.

Now there's the opening of the scene for this week. And I seem to be over my little tempest. I ought to apologize to you and to Dorothy for letting my inner woes get out like poison. I think I ruined your dinner last night. I didn't want to. And apology is no good. I didn't intend to. I don't know what causes it but every nerve end was on fire and little noises crashed on me like waves. I have not Elaine's gallantry. I should have been able to cover it up but I'm not that good. I wish I could reform but I know when this real nervous horror is on me I am helpless against it. So please believe that I am sorry. I think it is all over today. I hope it is. It is no new thing to me—a depression that destroys all the world. Women get it and since they have physical symptoms, it is an excuse. When a man gets it, he has no defense. And so I will only say, I was nervously sick all over. And I am sorry I could not control nor dissemble it. I hope it did not spoil the end of your vacation. It was not aimed at you. It came entirely out of me.

August 7, Tuesday

I felt very sad when your plane took off yesterday—felt a great sense of my own inadequacy. One of the troubles with being a specialized animal is that a normal life is abnormal and I am not very good at it. And I don't want to be protected in my shortcomings. Often then the shortcoming becomes a thing in itself. I'm glad we had the last talk though. I think it clarified some of the book things for you. And your worry about the Kate scene strikes a chord because it sounds false in my ears also.

Well, next week the birthday.* And I am going to miss a couple of days of work and the very sense of sin will be good for me. There's nothing like sin for the removal of complacency. But, I can't feel any complacency. There must be some though. There has to be. Anyway, the Japanese lanterns came and the boys and I will decorate the house early in the morning. And we will set up the presents and at 12 noon the salute. And at night a big beach picnic. That should be a birthday. And I do hope Elaine will like her presents. I just thought of another woman who could have had such a thing. The old dowager of China. But dowager means the country was ruled by council so she is out. No—there have been very few. Marie of Roumania was only regent. It's Victoria, Anne, Elizabeth, Mary, Mary of Scots (there's a new one but she didn't really rule either), Catherine of Russia and perhaps Isabella of Spain and that's the works since gunpowder. There were no queens of France or Germany or Italy or Spain except Isabella. Odd, isn't it. You think there are but there aren't. William and Mary—but he was the boss.

Well, I started the Dessie scene yesterday. Read it to Elaine last night and she likes it. In it there will be a rather terrible attempt to recreate the past. Nearly everyone tries it at one time or another and it always fails. The most terrible wrenching scene I can remember in my life was the Christmas after my mother was paralyzed. My father tried to make an old Christmas. We decorated a tree in her room and had presents and tried to make the Christmas jokes. And I remember her eyes—cold as marbles but alive. I don't know how much she could see or understand.

---

* Elaine's.

But it breaks me up every time I remember how hard my father tried. It's little wonder he didn't live long after she died. He had no heart for it. His spirit hung on him like the limp clothes on a scarecrow.

I have the bottom of the box just about hollowed down to the level I want. Must straighten the edges and make the bottom level and then just polish and polish. And when I get it home I will put the lamb's wool power buffer on it and it will glow. Elaine suggests making the jacket look like the box, like wood with the grain and the polish. I don't think anyone buys my books because of the color of the jacket. And surely the carved wood might be an unusual and striking thing. And now to work.

August 8, Tuesday

Violent rain and wind. And it looks like a storm of several days. This will make it a touch difficult to concentrate because the boys have to play in the house. And it is impossible for them to be quiet. Elaine, however, suggested cotton in the ears and I have tried it and it works so well that I am going to buy some ear plugs. Might make a great difference.

Went fishing yesterday afternoon and we caught 49 scups and had a lot of them for dinner last night. That's the kind of fishing I like. What a grey day, and really violent.

Now to book. I'm going to try to create a curious mood today. I won't tell you what it is. But I want to see if you can feel it. And the method will be one I developed long ago. Now I will see whether I will be able to use it. It's the roundabout method that seems so simple and is actually a choice of symbol blended with word sound. The intent is to soften resistance to the mood by the continuation of sounds and small pictures—miniscule things, about imperceptible. I don't know whether I can do it or not. It's a thing to try. And I am pretty sure I can do it. We will see.

Last night, after being on the water, we were so sleepy that we went to bed at 8:30 and slept before nine. The great wind and rain storm came up in the night. And I didn't even hear it until it was well along. My desk was flooded and my chair soaked. Fortunately there was no manuscript on my desk.

Tonight the masquerade for the kids, and ours are going as Three Blind Mice with bandaged tails and tin cups. They should be cute. We made the ears and tails the night before last. I hope it isn't as stormy as it is now. The rain is pouring down.

And I must go to work. I really must. And right at that moment I had an invention. And I haven't time to think of it. Now I must really go to work.

August 9, Thursday

Your letter about the salutes came yesterday. It will be 41 guns. That is accurate and sixty-two are too many. It will be just fine. But I'll give you a report on it. It will happen at high noon. Only one thing remains to come and it will probably be along. The boys and the boy next door went to the children's masquerade and won first prize as the funniest. They went as Three Blind Mice. They were very funny. Tamara Geva* comes today. She will not bother me. In fact she helps a lot with the kids. And my work will go right on. I am going to take two days off next week, however. Need it I think.

I hope you liked the scenes with Tom and Dessie. They are so very carefully done and I hope they are successful. It is the last of the Hamilton sequences. Only Will can come back. What really happened to Will is so silly that I cannot use it. His wife died. He married his stenographer. She got him to retire to golf and travel and he died of boredom in six months. It's too pat. I couldn't think of using it.

The rain yesterday was tremendous and today it is overcast but it will clear about noon I think. No, it is clearing now. And I must not forget to send you a check when I send mss. on Saturday. I will pin it to the script. I got the box hollowed but not polished. Probably finish all the rough work tonight. I've lost more weight around the middle. My pants fall off. And that's not a bad idea. I want to lose 10 more pounds and then I will be about right and try to stay there.

I feel funny today. Kind of excited and restless and good in a shivery way. This means nothing except that I have had enough rest. I guess that's it but it makes me feel prophetic of very fine things to come. I should be writing now. But for some reason I put it off for a while until my handwriting clears. I guess I am not ready yet.

Everyone who sees it falls in love with your box. And there

---

* The ballerina and actress.

is still lots of work to do on it. Lots. But if I get it done when the mss. is done, that will be time enough. It gives me lots of time. And I need lots of time.

Now the sun comes out. It is going to be a warm and lovely day. But I'll have to stay in and work. I can see it is going to be slow today—very slow. And I don't much care. It's funny—I am reluctant to start on the last book because it will mean I must go through to the end and I guess I don't want to finish this book. I don't want it finished. It will be a sad day for me when it is done. I have never loved my work more, in fact never as much. And I don't mean the finished work but the working. But now I guess I really must get to it.

August 10, Friday

Another week. I will not be able to finish the Tom and Dessie sequence and I wish I could, so that when I take the two days off I can start with something fresh. Maybe I'll work tomorrow. Surely I will work on Monday. That's it. That will be the finish of Tom.

Geva and Kent Smith* came last night. She will stay a few days but he goes tomorrow. Being thoughtful professional people, they are out for a long walk until I can get my work done. The fog is hanging very heavily this morning and the island is damp. The paper is a little clammy.

Now I will cut out the external things.

Today I have to do something I haven't done in this whole book. I have to eliminate some of yesterday's work and change the pace I had set for it. It has not been often. It was just wrong. But I don't mind. And surely that is a minimum.

I won't get it off to you until tomorrow because Elaine wants to read it tonight, but you will still get it Monday so that's all right too.

I guess I should go to it now.

August 12 [SUNDAY]

If I am late with the mss. this week, it is because I wanted to finish the section before Elaine's birthday. So I have worked into

---

* The actor who played the lead in *Burning Bright*. See footnote on page 153.

the week end and then I shall take three days off and I think I need it. The last part of the book is coming up. I want to be fresh for it. And I have been getting too tired toward the end of the week lately. Also the story of Tom and Dessie has taken toll of me. I don't know whether I have managed to project my feeling about it. It is so personal. Maybe no one else can feel it. I don't know. But here it is anyway. Let me know whether it is effective. At the very end I will leave the realistic and try to go into music again as I did with Samuel. But it will be a kind of counterpoint to his music and—well, we will see. Maybe good, maybe bad. But I shall want to draw the reader into the personal so that he is reading about himself.

Anyway, we will try it.

There it's done. And very unconventional. I'll wonder whether you like it. It tells an awful lot about Tom.

August 16, Thursday

This follows the longest layoff since I started the book. And I am very glad I took it for a number of reasons. First, I was tired. Second, I had finished a time, a mood and a section. And third, I needed a freshness for the last.

Now I go into the final book. And because it is an entirely new book, I am going to number the pages from #1 but this is only for myself because it will give me a sense of newness and freshness. I know it may be harder on the copyist but it will be easier on me.

The birthday was fine and I think my dear Elaine enjoyed it and surely you, Pat and Dorothy, contributed to it very largely. Geva is going home today. We have only one more guest and that is Liz* for a week end. I have one more month only. And I shall not be sad to go back to New York. I like my house and my tools. And in a month we will have had enough of this. It has been good, but good things should not last too long or they cease to be good things.

The boys have had a good summer. I really think Tom has improved some. I know what you mean about him. I feel his sadness too. And there is a double thing which I will one day discuss with you. I feel that the pattern of the last few years is

---

* Elizabeth Ainsworth, another of Steinbeck's nieces.

nearly over for all of us. [. . .] Its course is about run. And maybe we will do better in the next frame.

My health is good and a letter from Dr. Negrin tells me yours is too and that you have a very definite improvement—this gratuitously in a letter about other things. So—we go into the last phase with no health hazards.

The state of mind is good too, I think. It is not set in any direction at all, it is not bored nor anxious and particularly is it not in any hurry to be done. All this is of course a kind of evaluation before going into the final section. I feel able to go into it. And I am now ready to discuss it in notes. It amounts to a whole novel in subject matter. I think it will be in the neighborhood of 80,000 words. Maybe a few less. It has three preceding books to fulfill and resolve. It will continue and carry out the design of the earlier two books. I know most of its incidents. I think it will have power and development. Aron will develop to a certain extent but the powerful new people are Cal and Abra and a new Adam. And it is going to concentrate on them. The book has scattered a good deal. Now I feel that it must pull in tightly as it goes. All of the principles have been laid down except the principle of Abra. She is new to the book, the strong female principle of good as opposed to Cathy. Her strength will not be soft. Abra is a fighter and an effective human being. She will take active part in the battle. So—now we are about ready to go. We have a new kind of a world in the Salinas Valley and our timeless principles must face a new set of facts and react to them. Are you interested to see what happens? I am.

And now to go. And I don't know that any will go down today and I don't care.

August 20, Monday

Well I did what I intended. I took the whole week off and I succeeded for a couple of days in putting the whole book out of my mind. I don't know whether or not I was right. Only the next few weeks will tell. But it seemed to me that I needed it and so I took it. Now I am ready to go on with the last book and the only break will be the time when we move back to New York. And since that will be on a Sunday, it is probable that I may not lose any working time at all. Our reservation on the boat is for the morning of Sept. 16. And I have several weeks before then.

I still think it good to treat this last book as a unit even to pagination. However, we will have to see about that. The book will take its own pace, as I have said so often. We will see.

Naturally, having lost the rhythmic discipline, I shall be in trouble for the first day or two but that will be all right too. How the mind rebels against work, but once working, it rebels just as harshly against stopping. I don't know why this should be. It's a dumb brute, the human mind. And it has really brutish tendencies.

I am going to open this book with a kind of a refrain. You will recognize it with the second line I think. And I know it is proper for design. It is the recapitulation of intention. And I do know that just before your final stream—one should pause to re-establish what the pattern was in the mind of the reader. And this is what I intend to do or try to.

My mind is letting in all kinds of side things from the world of my life. That is how quickly discipline is lost. It happens very soon. And I must shake my spirit like a rag. And I will.

I am thinking about Tom. We, and particularly Elaine, have done good things for him this summer but there is much more to do—much more. And we will try our best to work out what we can.

Now—I am going to wipe out the world of my life and get into the opening of the last of the book. And for this purpose I am going to start on a fresh, free page.

There I have finished the opening of Book 4. And it is a refrain of the opening of the century. And I have ranged the changeable with the continuing. Also I have set down some things which I believe and some things which have not been said for a long time and which should be said and must be said, particularly since they are true.

August 21, Tuesday

Well, I opened Book 4 yesterday with general statement and also with specific statement which can only be known when one finishes the book. I think when Harold says the book is ambitious he doesn't know how ambitious it is. Only you and I and Elaine know that. And maybe we are the only ones who will ever know it. It has things in it which will probably never come out because readers do not inspect very closely and when they do, like as not they find things which aren't there. The hell with it. I'll just do my work and forget everything else.

Less than a month now. Our reservation on the boat is for the morning of the 16th which is Sunday, a bad day to travel but the only reservation we could get around that time. It means we move on a week end again so I will not lose much if any time from work. We think we will send Louise in a couple of days ahead of us on the train so she can get the house in running order and have it clean and lived-in looking and feeling.

Waverly is supposed to arrive the 26th. I hope this is so but nothing planned there is dependable. But it would be good if she could come and have a few weeks with us.

My mind is wandery this morning. I know what I am going to write and why I am going to write it in this place but you don't. I think you will be pleased though. And I'm glad you found the Tom and Dessie part effective. I don't want this book to have an overtone of sorrow any more than it exists in the world itself. I want Sam Hamilton to be remembered with pleasure, not thought of sadly. And the opening of Book 4 is not light and airy. The balance of everything has to be maintained. And so I am going to begin Book 4 with Lee. I think that will please you but that is not why I am doing it. It pleases my sense of design and proportion. And so I will get to it.

August 22, Wednesday

A damp, windy, sticky really nasty day—perhaps the worst we have had. Clothes are clammy and have an odor. Kids are irritable. I hope it breaks tonight. Also I think it is only bad in Nantucket terms. It would be fine and pleasant in New York. And as I said that, the sun broke through. Isn't that nice? I can do my work today with the forecast that it will be sunny. I hope you liked the work yesterday, Lee's departure and return. Elaine liked it because it made her laugh and cry at the same time. I thought I might go to San Francisco with Lee. But there would be no point in it. This book doesn't need richness now. It needs tightness, story, character and to a certain extent, speed. I am looking forward to the work today. It will be quite different from anything you have ever read on the subject. And I just hope I can make you believe it. And I think I can. And because this part is a very important part, it is going to be longer because—

naive as it may sound—all hell is going to break loose in a character sense and things very very important to the book.

As Lee said yesterday, I think adults forget about children. They just literally do not remember how it was. I think I do remember and I am going to try very hard to remember more.

And now I am about ready to go.

August 23, Thursday

Now the book begins to move again. Please watch the development of Aron's character. It is most important to the story but its development will be very gradual and I hope subtle. Also, please watch Abra. She is terribly important also. God almighty, this is a complicated book. I wonder whether I can do it. I know what you mean about two volumes. I'm on it all the time. But I wouldn't live any other way. Weather has cleared up now and I hope we will have a few weeks of nice weather. After my week off, I am glad to be back at work. The typescript came and I glanced through it. Pretty good in places, quite good but needs lots of delicate cleaning-up work. Well I will do it.

You know after the summer and boys and play and the days being too short, I am glad that my last 30,000 words will be done in New York. There won't be any distractions there. And I'll want full concentration for my ending. But I seem to be able to concentrate pretty well even here.

From the number of pages I guess my estimate was pretty accurate—between 240,000 and 250,000 words.

I do hope you like the return of Lee. I think it is pretty good and short enough. I need Lee, not only as an interpreter but as an active figure. I have a feeling of goodness about the book now but there is so much to come, I don't for the life of me know how I got in what I have already.

On an impulse I just went back and read the opening notes addressed to you. I wanted to see whether I had failed in any part to carry out my intention and I do not think I have. The direction has not changed a bit and this book which seems to sprawl actually does not at all. It is almost as tight as a short story. And I am pleased about that.

Now—I have a little over three weeks left here. Elaine has more mss. here than she can ever get done before we leave. Therefore, I think you should not send any more mss. here, either original or typescript. Keep it there. Of course, as always, I will send you the week's work as I finish it. And do you realize that after this week, there will only be three more 10's—40,000 words nearly, counting this week's work. And about one more month in town will finish it. I really should go to work now but I am putting it off. It is quite early. Elaine is going to take the boys to a movie this afternoon and then they are coming back and we are all going out to dinner. So I have all day at my desk and I like that. I feel so good today—just wonderful. I have a kind of soaring joyousness. And now I would engage your prayers for me because I am going to try to go into the minds of children, but more than that, I am going to try to set those minds down on paper. And these are not children as they are conceived by adults but children as they are to and among themselves. I hope I can do that. Most of what I read about children is crap. Grown people forget. They feel that at a certain age they got insight and aware- ness and wisdom. And as a rule the opposite is true to a certain extent. And so I will set it down and I think it will be an unique record of the thinking of children. And I think it will be accurate at least of my characters. And children are no more alike than are adults.

Thursday, August 23, Later

I got half my day's work done and the kids off to a movie and then cut my thumb closing a balky knife. My right thumb too, dam it. I bled it and bound it and it will heal in a couple of days but it makes it a little hard to write and maybe it will be hard to read too. I hope not. I'll be very careful to try to keep it legible.

Now I will go back to the second half of my day's work and please believe me that this is not too grown up. It is exactly the way 11-year-olds might talk and act. People just forget.

August 24, Friday

Clumsy handwriting again because of the bandage. But this was a deep true cut with a sharp knife and it was a good bleeder. I did not touch any water nor disinfective to it. I let the blood flow for a while and then cinched the edges tight together. Then last night I covered it with penicillin and I think by Mon- day it will be practically gone. The only trouble now is the clum- siness of the bandage. But I will write slowly and carefully and try to be legible. And I'll put the first week's mss. in the mail today. And I hope you will like it. This last part is very important. It may sound like children but it is children who will be adults.

Why do men do things which seem off pattern? I don't think they do. I think if you look back in a man's life you will find both a cause and a parallel. People do not change very much. Now in the whole of this book Aron is not as important as Cal but he is surely as important in the sense that he is a catalyst of Cal. And so we must know about the nature of the catalyst. And that is what I am more or less working on today. I think you know Cal so far better than you know Aron. And I am going to try to remedy that. And now

August 24, Friday, continued

There's the first week of the last book done. Careful as it is, I'm afraid it might seem disappointing to you. The end of the last book was a series of crises, stimulating and violent. And now I have to go back and build again. And your taste for violence might possibly be aroused so that it will sound dull. But there must be lulls and this must be built again from the ground up. Well, you'll just have to take it. Let me hear from you. Suddenly I feel lonely in a curious kind of way. I guess I am afraid. That always comes near the end of a book—the fear that you have not accomplished what you started to do. That is as natural as breathing, and so—the week.

August 27, Monday

Here goes the summer. Waverly arrived yesterday and very tired and glad to be here. I have to get back to my job now and I am sadly confused. This is my own fault. I have slipped some way through tiredness or because perhaps old wounds broke open. I guess things never heal completely. Well, the job is to get back on some kind of an even keel and finish out the summer. I have exactly three weeks more here. And I would like to have thirty more pages to show for it. I probably will have, too, but the quality—that must stay up. This is the time in a book when worry sets in. There should be no objective attack on the book yet. It must keep striking out from the inside until the last word is written. So I am cheating now by evaluating. We have had our last guest now and our last party gone too and I feel really beaten to a pulp. But I'll come back quickly I think. I always have. I suppose there will come a time when I do not. This would be a bad time for that. Such a strange way to live. But then I guess there is no way that is not strange. It is very odd, almost what the French call a *crise de nerfs*. I'm crawling with them today. Well, I'll fight that off. Have to.

In the book I have reached a place of great difficulty. You see I want to make a lunge forward in time for the sake of design and still I want to maintain an even steady flow. These two don't go together very well. I'll have to work it out. And I will of course. Perhaps the best way is the most direct way. And you know, all this might well be a deep psychic cry of laziness finding channels of escape from work. I think I will go after it on that basis. Heaven knows I've got plenty of it. My brain just doesn't want to tackle it today and if I let it get away with it, tomorrow it will have another excuse. My brain is very treacherous and I do not dare to give it any freedom to wander.

Now the time is coming for the test—whether I will be able to master it or whether it will win over me. We'll just have to see and I think I will start now and see who wins.

Later. Well there you have it. It is the change in Adam. I hope it isn't dull. You must know that refrigeration was the reason for the great change in the Valley. And out of that Valley came a large part of the pioneering which has changed the food supply of the world. And the crazy thing is that the men who worked at it first all failed. But there's the beginning of it.

August 28, Tuesday

Yesterday was a very bad day as you may have noticed and yet what I put in was necessary. I do not want Adam to be merely an onlooker at his time, to prop him up in front of a deck of years. He has to have a part in its development. It is a difficult section for me, so I will get to it very soon. Yesterday we caught a bucket of crabs. Very good. We will go after some more today I think. Now if the book can only go as well as the summer.

The Log* came and it is a very good-looking book. It

---

* *Log from the Sea of Cortez* was published separately in September 1951.

would not seem to me that it would sell very well but these are curious times. I think it will in Europe. And it is barely possible that it might catch on a little here. When, I wonder, does it come out? It is a curious time for books. People do seem to like thoughtfulness—or do they? Maybe they only want reassurance or sensation.

Now to work.

August 29, Wednesday

There's a real feeling of finality in the air here. We have two weeks and a half more so it is not as near as I seem to indicate but the fall is surely coming. And I have an autumn feeling in me. This is one of the best feelings I know. I have always loved the fall. No reason. It is filled with a warm sweet sadness which is close relative to pleasure and not very far removed. We have had a good and productive summer. The boys have made a great jump I think. It is hard to see if you are with them every day but I am sure it is so.

I have dawdled away a good part of my free time now carving vaguely on a scrap of mahogany, but I guess I have been thinking too. Who knows. I sit here in a kind of a stupor and call it thought.

Now let's stop this and get to the story. It has progressed pretty well this week. What seems kind of accidental is not. I don't think there is a single sentence in this whole book that does not either develop character, carry on the story or provide necessary background. I think that is so but I'll have to see when I am done. I don't want a wandering book and I think this one does not. My god, it can't. There isn't time. And I'd better stop wandering too.

August 30, Thursday

Here we go again and I feel somewhat easier than I did. I got your letter with the enclosures yesterday. The British didn't like Burning Bright* any more than the Americans did. I guess I was wrong but I'm still glad I did it.

Another white night last night and that's two in a row.

---

* Steinbeck's short novel (1950), later produced as a play, on the theme of sterility.

But the next section is so intricate that I get to thinking about it at night. It is not only complex psychologically but also in a story sense. And I must sort it out and make it seem very simple. We have two weeks from Sunday and I am going to try to get a full week's work done each week.

Now I think I had better get to work. And in this next every line is important.

August 30 [31], Friday

Another week and really we moved on this week even if it did not seem to. Now only two more weeks of work before we go back to New York. We were talking this morning about the summer. We have been out only about two times not counting the times when you were here and you know what that was. We have made a custom of having a couple of drinks before dinner which is good for me. It relaxes and soothes. I have been fairly nervous several times and always due to the same thing—a tearing or splitting of thought. I simple can't do two things at once and an attempt at it makes me very nervous. But the work has got done whether good or bad. And none of us know that and won't for some time. I'm glad you like the things about the children. I have always felt that, except for Hughes,* children were badly written. They have been underwritten.

I will not finish any sequence today. There is much too much of it and it seems to me to be very important. And so I must take it slowly and I must do it very well. I must admit that I am becoming a little timid as the book progresses. It is fear that I am not accomplishing what I want to. I guess that is inevitable. I'll have to take stock now pretty soon and that is difficult with all the mix-up of closing out the summer, but there it is to do. And I will do it too—believe me. I will draw on some reservoir of will and get it done. Always do—always. And that's one of the worst lies I ever told. It's a strange world I am making but one I think is true and beyond that I cannot go.

I will be glad to be back in New York. I seem to have more time there. Isn't that strange? But it is because I feel a responsibility to be with my boys as much as I can. Tom has had another flare-up but I think it will very quickly get solved. We know now when they come even if we do not know entirely why.

---

* Richard Hughes, author of *A High Wind in Jamaica*.

154

September 3, Monday

I think it is time for me to get on with my work now.

Labor Day today and for me the term could be used in its most strenuous and biologic sense. This is a blue day full of fears and little weeping clouds. Writing is a very silly business at best. There is a certain ridiculousness about putting down a picture of life. And to add to the joke—one must withdraw for a time from life in order to set down that picture. And third one must distort one's own way of life in order in some sense to simulate the normal in other lives. Having gone through all this nonsense, what emerges may well be the palest of reflections. Oh! it's a real horse's ass business. The mountain labors and groans and strains and the tiniest of rodents comes out. And the greatest foolishness of all lies in the fact that to do it at all, the writer must believe that what he is doing is the most important thing in the world. And he must hold to this illusion even when he knows it is not true. If he does not, the work is not worth even what it might otherwise have been. As it says in The King and I —"Is a mystery!"*

All this is a preface to the fear and uncertainties which clamber over a man so that in his silly work he thinks he must be crazy because he is so alone. If what he is doing is worth doing—why don't more people do it? Such questions. But it does seem a desperately futile business and one which must be very humorous to watch. Intelligent people live their lives as nearly on a level as possible—try to be good, don't worry if they aren't, hold to such opinions as are comforting and reassuring and throw out those which are not. And in the fullness of their days they die with none of the tearing pain of failure because having tried nothing they have not failed. These people are much more intelligent than the fools who rip themselves to pieces on nonsense. And with that I will go to work. Two more weeks of it before I go into New York. Twenty more pages and I will be at my own writing board. And I will be glad to be there.

September 4, Tuesday

Yesterday was very bad as I guess the notes will indicate. I had a vision of human personality as a kind of foetid jungle

---

* The much-quoted phrase from *The King and I* was, "Is a puzzlement!"

full of monsters and daemons and little lights. It seemed to me a dangerous place to venture, a little like those tunnels at Coney Island where "things" leap out screaming. Think the work was good yesterday. But it was painful. And I guess that is because it was true. And what happens today will be true too. It's a kind of a terrible part of the book but there are a great many terrible parts. Maybe it is a terrible book. We'll just have to see. I have been accused so often of writing about abnormal people. I don't feel that these are with the one exception of Cathy. And that is not a great proportion—one in so many. And she will be more and more understandable I think as it goes on. I just don't know when it is going to stop. I can't rush it now because everything that happens is important to the book. But, hell, that's one of my problems now which I didn't have earlier. I am at least in my mind interfering with the pace instead of letting it find its own. And that I simply must stop. The scene I have to write today is very strange. I don't want to make it less strange but I do want to make it very convincing. And the best way to do that is to put most of it in dialogue. I think this week's work is going to excite you. I hope it does. It is very different because it deals with tiny nodes of character which are nevertheless very powerful in what is to happen.

September 5 [WEDNESDAY]

A very late start but I have it very well thought out today. Weather is superb, really lovely but no longer summer weather. It is definitely fall. And it feels good to the skin. People are herding off the island going back to their jobs and we still have a week and a half. It will I hope be a productive week for me.

The scene I am on is of utmost importance. In it you see a man growing up and a woman growing old. And I hope I am getting it over. The best thing for me to do would be to get it written and then discuss it and so I will.

September 6, Thursday

Only ten more days here, or rather only nine. It is nearly over and the usual story of ups and downs with many more ups than down. At least I believe that to be true. I guess the most important thing to you and to a large extent to me is the fact that the work has not stopped except for the week when I wanted it to stop. To a very great extent that is Elaine's doing since she took over and handled the things which might have interfered and did it so well that I could give much of my thought to the writing. I will admit that the boys and especially Tom's trouble have been a difficulty to me and a haunting thing which has bothered me particularly because I can't do anything much about it. But I am surely going to try.

As to the work itself, only time will show whether it has been good. Sometimes it seems to me actually to have the high purpose I set for it, and at other times it seems pedestrian and trite. I know how much work must go into it after it is done but I have plenty of time for that and I am quite willing to do it. This is *the* Book still as far as I am concerned and I think it will continue to be until it is finally in your hands. Then of course there will be another book or a funeral. I think if I were forbidden by some force to work, I should last a very short time. And I don't say that morbidly at all. I think perhaps I am one of those lucky mortals whose work and whose life are the same thing. It is rare and fortunate.

I got the return card yesterday so I know that last week's mss. got through to your manger Labor Day. I hope you liked it. I am pretty sure that you will like this week's work. I feel that it is subtle and good, and also, the threads begin to draw in like the first tug on the guide lines of a purse seine to bring all the fish gradually in together. But, Pat, there's so much to come— so very much.

And I must get to work now. The children are unusually noisy today and I haven't the heart to make them stop. There is a little boy next door who is the noisiest of all. But he goes home tomorrow, thank God. Waverly is being wonderful not only in the house but in her relationship with the kids. She is really taking hold as the older sister which is all the more remarkable because she has no training at it.

Finally in my dawdle period—the scene for today. I think it may make your flesh crawl a little. But it is part of the inevitable development.

And now I will get to it.

September 7, Friday

Now another week and they seem to pop up like ducks in a shooting gallery. There is one more week of work after today. I'll pack in the evenings and on Saturday. I will be glad to get home. It has been a real fine summer.

There isn't any point in going over details. So I will go directly into work notes.

This week has been a hard one. I have put the forces of evil against a potential good. Yesterday I wrote the outward thing of what happened. Today I have to show what came of it. This is quite different from the modern hard-boiled school. I think I must set it down. And I will. The spots of gold on this page are the splatterings from beautiful thoughts.

Well, Pat, there is the end of this week's work. I hope you will like it. I believe that the beginning of disintegration is logical and sound. I only hope it is effective.

Next week will be a crucial week in the story. And I will send it or bring it in with me. I don't know which. Anyway, I'm a little tired. The week has wearied me a great deal. And there have been other things, which I will tell you when I see you. So long for now.

September 10, Monday

Now into the last week. It is not strange that my sense of time has been lifted out of weeks and months and days and is now felt in units of ten pages of mss. If I can send you on Friday page 40 of this series, I shall be glad. I was interested in your letter about the interview between Cal and Lee. You must never quite believe that I am putting myself down on paper or if you do so believe, you must never say so. There are many things which must not be said but which must be translated into symbols. Robinson Jeffers once said that he wrote witches and devils outside the house in order to prevent their getting in the house. Maybe everyone does that to a certain extent. But again we must not mistake mouse mutterings for earthquakes. That would be a bad mistake.

Elizabeth Otis writes that perhaps this book has grown in conception since I started it. And I wonder whether that is so. I planned it as a huge thing. I have been afraid that it narrowed down from the big thing rather than expanded. As a matter of fact I've wondered whether it was not becoming little. I want it large. What I would like would be for it to read little but to leave a vast feeling. And about that I can't tell. It is only what I hope.

Now I must get to it. The episodes of this week stem from the other things of the last two weeks. And my hope is that I can conceal my symbol until the very last and make it only come flashing in when the whole episode is over. We will see whether or not I can do that. The next two weeks contain some of the most important work to be done.

September 11, Tuesday

A brilliant beautiful day and I am so nervous I can't sit still. I can't imagine why. Maybe a weariness but more likely complications of moving, all kinds of side issues and trying to keep work going too. I get confused. And that is probably it. I can't imagine what else.

Louise goes back to New York tonight to open and clean the house. And I will be very glad to have that done even though it means we do all the work here the rest of the week. I'll do the packing at night. It's quite a job to move a whole family. Of course Elaine does the great part of it, the planning, etc. But I'll be glad when it is done.

My work today is interesting to me. It sounds simple but it isn't. And I think I will get to it now.

There, Pat, that part is done. And do you think it is good? Can you see its motivation? And don't think I'm making this up. This is exactly how it was done.

September 12, Wednesday

Three more days of work here. And very important days too. The move and one of the major climaxes of the book come at the same time. But this is not abnormal. Things always happen like that. It is a real tough piece of work to come. This is a most complicated climax because it is a quadruple climax—most difficult because it must be very clear and clean. Also it is a climax not only of event but of emotion. Out of it two lives are lost and two changed, maybe more than this, so you can see that I am approaching this with trepidation and I wish I didn't have moving to think about, but in the long run I don't think it makes very much difference. One works. That is a verity. One does work.

When I get home I am going to put new blotters on my writing table and sharpen absolutely new pencils and open a new case of paper and I'll be going into the last part of the book. And God knows how long that will take. I just really don't know in spite of my brave words about Oct. first. I just don't know. It stretches on and on and I hope it is still interesting. That I do hope. I have wondered whether these people could become tiresome. But I think they have enough versatility not to be repetitive or tedious. Well I guess I have taken up as much time as possible .

Now it is time to get to it.

September 13, Thursday

Great weariness is in me, so thoroughly mixed as to be almost imperceptible but I am honeycombed with it. I must ignore it.

The book draws into its last part now and I suppose it is only sporting to rattle a little. I shall welcome criticism of method or technique but this book is no more a collaboration than any of the others have been. The morals, ideas, philosophies are my own and are not offered for correction or revision. That is no change. It is just a restatement to save time.

I have only today's work and tomorrow's before I go home. And I think I won't write any more notes today. There's a towering black cloud with thunder in it.

September 24, Monday

Now—back to work after a week off. More than that—a week and a day. I didn't realize how tired I had got but I know it now by contrast. I am all rested now. The week did fine things for me and I am full of piss and vinegar again.

This is not to say it is going to be easy. It will be hard to go to work today—hard to get back the rhythm and drive and direction—but at least I will have the energy for it. And I am looking forward to it very much. I can't work all the time but I should. The conditioned animal again. Always the conditioned animal.

The pagination of this manuscript is strange. I am going

to start at #1 again and this time I hope it will go on through to the end. If it ever gets done, and I have no idea that it ever will, I will be just lucky.

In the country I always tried to get finished so I could play with the boys. Now I can take my time in finishing and as a change I like that.

Very hard to start—very hard—perhaps impossible.

September 25 [TUESDAY]

As you will very well see, I didn't finish my full day of work yesterday. I told you on the phone it was hard getting started again, not for what to say but to re-establish the rhythm. But I don't worry. It will go on in spite of my derelict qualities. In this book I am a bystander and I know it. The book goes on. I do hope you like the account of how war came to Salinas. It is true.

Story: A friend has just sent me a book he wrote asking for a quote. I gave it to Elaine and last night she told me about it and read me some of it. And it is very bad. Can't write, can't think and has nothing to say. I'm sorry and perhaps it is mean but I feel better about my own book. I was in a slump but my book is better than that one on all counts.

Rainy day today and the sky dark. To me a pleasant kind of day. My mood is not dour but I love the weeping sky. I seem also to be very corny today. Hope it doesn't get into my work. Real cliché-rid today. Well must stop it. But I think I will have only four days' work this week and I don't even care about that. What rebellion is here. What courage, what originality. And now I am going to get to it.

Now, my work is done for today and it is a full day's work. I think you can see what I am preparing and also I am about ready to go into Abra. And I feel very good about the whole thing because now it is going to move toward its next climax. And I am shivery about that. Well, we'll see what tomorrow will bring.

September 26, Wednesday

Well here we go again. The week is very busy and I am not at ease with it but will make it all right I'm pretty sure. Change

of tempo has something to do with it I guess. Bound to. Play*
opening tonight downtown. All of these things impinge a little
but I'll get through o.k. But I do feel strange—almost unearthy.
I'll never get quite used to being alive. It's a mystery. Always
startled to find I have survived.

The beautiful cool fall weather which I adore going on
right outside my window. I don't feel lazy at all. It's just fine.
What a busy place New York is. I must get a new desk blotter.
This has a crease in the middle which bothers me.

Stalling—stalling over the bounding main. I haven't the
proper face for glasses. They never quite fit. I think I will have
to remake some so they do. Always slipping off. Now I should
be ready. I've left Abra in the kitchen with Lee and we'll have
to go back there and find them. It is quiet but an important day
in the mss. I want to take a good deal of time with it. And then
I have another scene before climax for this section. But all in
good time. It all takes time. I need so much time to waste also.
Seem to require about 4 to 1 of waste over work.

September 27, Thursday

Last night we saw the good production of Burning Bright
which seemed better for its poverty. I enjoyed it but I think my
weariness came from confusion. I seem capable of great effort in one direction but given a confusion of ends, I collapse.
And today time is a wasting and I must go to work.

September 28, Friday

This is a beat-up week. And I hope there aren't more like
it. Split interests have destroyed me. Ideally, I should have
finished my book in the country and come in only to correct.
But it didn't work that way. And it couldn't. This week I have
begun to work toward a climax of this part and next week I
hope to get past that climax. But next week will not have a play
in it. I didn't really get going this week. You will find only four
days of work if that.

---

* Burning Bright.

October 1, Monday

This book seems fated to be done with a counterpoint of small, rather funny frustrations. The woman who rented my apartment has run off sans rent and ruined the walls. I could hire someone to fix it over but I can do it myself more quickly and better. So I will go there, prepare it this afternoon, and tomorrow I will paint it. There is always something. Always will be too. For I truly believe that people call their lives to them the way you'd whistle up a dog. I seem to thrive in small frustrations and make them when I don't have them. This is not abnormal. In fact it is very supernormal.

I am stuck this morning because I don't know exactly where I am and what was in the work. You aren't in your office. Of course I know you are out for coffee. But I will have trouble starting until I can talk to you. But that's all right. Today's story is one of almost animal double-dealing, but double-dealing so natural that it is not even dishonest to the people involved. It is hard to balance what we call the honest and decent against the dishonest and indecent because they are very much alike except in their ends. I suppose self-interest is the end of all. It is only the quality of the interest that is different. So I had better go to work.

October 2 [TUESDAY]

This is an interesting part of the story to me because in this important phase of two dishonest people trying to cheat each other, I have another microcosm. The fact that Joe acts wrongly doesn't make his act any different. He simply makes a mistake. His motives never change from simple self-interest.

Now I have finished this day's work. Had to work early. There's something I have to do this afternoon. I'll tell you about it maybe tomorrow. If it warrants telling by then. And now I'm going to get some abrasive to finish the top of your box.

October 3, Wednesday

Today Giants and Dodgers play off their tie. Today I must paint that damned apartment and today I'll go right on working. There is a kind of inevitable quality about this book. It just seems to stagger on. To work very early this morning. I hope to get to my work at painting very early. Tomorrow I am going to the opening of the World Series. I'll get up early and see how much I can get done in the morning. Maybe not much but some.

October 4, Thursday, 5:30 A.M.

Up and to my desk very early because going to the opening of the World Series today and I don't want to lose any work time. Baseball yesterday, probably the best game I or anyone ever saw.* And I was glad then that I had a full day of work in.

It is my opinion that I shall finish my book in three weeks beginning on Monday next. I am fairly sure that it will not be longer than that. Can't get used to the idea. It seems so strange. I read the last three days' work to Elaine last night. I guess this kind of viciousness is going to make you very nervous but it is the balance, a kind of delicate balance. There will always be the difficulty that the average reader is more interested in evil than in good. That is strange but it seems to me to be true.

Now I am going to work.

October 5, Friday

This is a hard week now nearly over. To survive this one is a job. I am mixed up with things. And the silly truth is that I can take almost any amount of work but I have very little tolerance for confusion. That throws me soon and hard. But as of today that will be over. Now that I can see the end of this work, and I think three more weeks will do it, a great change is coming over me. I am reluctant to finish. But do you know—the decision to do a second volume dealing with the second 30 years has made a great difference. This means that I am not finished. I guess I am terrified to write finish on the book for fear I myself will be finished. The second volume puts it off quite a bit. Isn't that fine? I am almost gay about it. And I had better be gay because I am coming into the most violently emotional scene I have ever attempted and I am frankly afraid of it. For, while it must explode with emotion, it must also be restrained in treatment. Almost as though the reader brought his own pocket full of emotion to the

---

* The Giants beat the Dodgers 5-4, with a three-run homer by Bobby Thomson when they were trailing 4-2, in the third game of their play-off for the National League pennant. They lost the World Series to the Yankees.

page. I wish I could do this well. Today of course I am going to end the slower organ music and get ready for the announcement of the end. The end will be announced very soon now. And heaven knows I am afraid. It's a new thing and a strange thing and a frightening thing. The incident of Mr. Fenchel the tailor is exactly true. That is even his name. Mary* remembers it too and with the same shrinking kind of shame.

October 7, Sunday

World Series rained out today so I think I will try to get some work done. Will try anyway. I have a powerful pain in the right pleural section but probably just the change of weather and it will be gone. I hope so because it is very inconvenient for breathing and makes for a kind of weariness. But I'm a mass of that anyway—very deep-seated. Lots of contributing factors, largely confusion, and some of it fear of endings. But, as was said very early in this book, one foot in front of the other and little by little. That's the only way to do it. Little by little. What a strange thing is a book. Sometimes I feel so close to it and sometimes very far away. Sometimes I love it and sometimes I hate it. I guess all of this is weariness. I dread the next scene very much. It is such a difficult one. So hard to do. And the longer I put it off

October 8, Monday, 6 A.M.

Yesterday's game was rained out (World Series). I did my day's stint and so got a little ahead. This morning got up at 5 and will get done again, I hope, and go to the game and again tomorrow. I guess the rain is over but it was a big one. The thunder and lightning last night and the pouring rain made for good and early sleeping.

This morning I looked at the Saturday Review, read a few notices of recent books, not mine, and came up with the usual sense of horror. One should be a reviewer or better a critic, these curious sucker fish who live with joyous vicariousness on other men's work and discipline with dreary words the thing which feeds them. I don't say that writers should not be disciplined, but I could wish that the people who appoint themselves to do it were not quite so much of a pattern both physically and mentally.

---

* His other sister, Mrs. W. N. Decker, who lived in Carmel, California.

I'll have to phone you this morning not to come over for book this afternoon. I shall not be here. The pain in the pleura is gone this morning thank goodness. Just a small cold no doubt but it hurt.

Now—the work. Because it is very early in the morning, I am looking for something to complain about. And there isn't anything really except that it is very early in the morning. Did you like yesterday's work? I thought the funeral of the nigger was pretty good and of course it keyed in the other thing, crazy Alf and Joe's access to rumors. The whole sequence will be completed today. Oh! Lord, there's so much of it that I can't leave out. So much. I guess I'd better get to it. It is daylight now and time to work.

October 9, Tuesday, 5:30 A.M. (again)

This will be the last of the very early starts. We have no tickets after today's game. It has been exciting but for me at least it will be enough. But I would not have missed it. Cold this morning. The winter is here or a junior relative of it. I am up very early so I won't have to rush it. The next scenes are terribly important to the book. I want them to be good and I want them to be very clear. And at the same time not belabored. Anyway, this set of scenes is going to tie into the end of the book.

It is a lovely clear cold day—the kind I love. I should finish early. I know what it's going to be like pretty much but even for me, there are sometimes surprises. There are four relationships to go through and probably all in today's work. And that is a lot. It will be well if I get to the work immediately.

October 10, Wednesday

Went to our last ball game yesterday and this morning slept until 9. And that seemed to have slept me out. I can't sleep indefinitely I find but also I don't ever get quite enough. And maybe that's the way I function best. If, that is, I can be said to function at all. Sometimes I wonder. I seem to exist on the lip of a curving wave—always seeming to be waiting for it to break from under me. And maybe that is enough of generality, except for one thing—

I have noticed so many of the reviews of my work show a

fear and a hatred of ideas and speculations. It seems to be true that people can only take parables fully clothed with flesh. Any attempt to correlate in terms of thought is frightening. And if that is so, East of Eden is going to take a bad beating because it is full of such things.

I don't really know how much I can do today. I'm a day ahead and perhaps I may just think. I have lots to think about in this final two weeks and a half. I may not have it done then. Can't tell. There's lots to do but I can't tell whether that lots is long or not until I come to it.

In a short time that will be done and then it will not be mine any more. Other people will take it over and own it and it will drift away from me as though I had never been a part of it. I dread that time because one can never pull it back, it's like shouting good-bye to someone going off in a bus and no one can hear because of the roar of the motor.

Now I have this Thanksgiving dinner coming up. And I want not to write it. Isn't that odd. I must admit that I have liked this book. Or at least I have liked being with it—living with it and going along with it. It will be like coming out into another world to finish it. And it might be a very good thing that there is another volume in prospect.

This day is going to be wasted in vagueness, I can see that.

I just haven't got it today. There's a sadness all over everything and the little mental plans do not come off. I don't have this very often but I surely have it today. I just don't.

October 11, Thursday

Last night to bed at 8:30 and slept nearly 11 hours in a kind of disgusted exhaustion with many bad dreams thrown in for good measure. All in all I had the sleep and am rested but groggy. So I will get to my work early and see what I can make of it. Our discussion yesterday is evidence of a ridiculous situation and one we will not permit to happen again—mainly the critical appraisal of a book which is not finished. I don't know how we got into this but we won't again. And there won't be any trouble about this. I'm pretty sure I can control it. My job now is just to finish it, not to defend it.

My job even more is to be sure it is well done in my own terms and to forget the rest. The time passes and I must pass with it. Today's work is one of those hazards we avoid as long as possible. One of the difficult times. But there are many. This is only one of them.

October 12, Friday

Also the day one Cristobal Colon is said to have discovered San Salvador Island. To me, so far, it is only Friday and I will have two days without work. This week has been a struggle. The scene is difficult and I don't know whether or not I have it. It is a preposterous situation for one thing. But is not all good literature preposterous? I think so. A situation is not written about until it becomes preposterous.

I feel good today. And I think I will do good work. I'd better. I want to very much. And this might be called the payoff scene. I think it is the key scene of all. Maybe that is why I have been so much afraid of it. But two nights of long and restful sleep have put me in a position of inner security so that I think I can finally do it.

There is only one thing to discuss. I have, during this whole writing, been doing something that is not good. You have been getting the week's work on Friday. This means that on Monday, when I am two days away from it, I do not have the last day's work to refer to. If, on the other hand, you were to get it on Monday, I would have the beginning of the week done with reference to the last. I don't know why I didn't think of this before. But I didn't. And I guess that is all for the notes today and I will go into the scene I have worried about. We shall see.

October 13, Saturday

I didn't quite finish the scene yesterday because I was very weary and I want fresh force for it. So I am up very early this morning having awakened normally thinking about the scene. It requires a very quiet force in complete control. I think I have that now. At least I am content that I have and we will have to see.

I'll write it now.

October 15, Monday

Again we start on the week. Last week I worked on Saturday because I wanted to finish the scene between Cal and Aron.

168

It had been with me a long time. I'm glad I finished it and I shall want to know whether or not you find it effective. It should have a dreadful quality of happening in spite of anything that could be done. It's what I have been aiming at for so many pages. It is a shock finally to come to it.

Now—you will be calling pretty soon or I will call you. I am going to finish my stint and then I want to go out to buy some things we need and to look at some things. Maybe you would like to go with me. We'll talk of that when I see you or rather talk to you. Today's work is half funny and it will be easy after that other. It was very difficult. I still think I will probably have my first draft done a week from next Friday. It seems that way anyway. Then Elaine and I are going away for a few days—alone and probably under an assumed name. I think I will need that. And now I have several very short sharp scenes to do and I might just as well get to them.

October 16 [TUESDAY]

I will be a little slow today because I didn't finish yesterday so I am up early to try to get it done. And I hope I shall. Today, I have a kind of a fairy tale to tell. I've wondered about it a good deal and I am fairly sure it is ready. Everyone will find something in himself of this, I think. I should like to finish with Kate today if I can. And I think I can.

I hope you liked last week's work—some of the hardest in the whole book. Today's story is pretty good I think.

October 16, Tuesday, continued

I didn't tell you that I got up at four this morning to work on this final Cathy scene—but I did. Couldn't sleep for thinking about it and I couldn't see any reason to lie in bed waiting for daylight. I guess there will be a howl that I am being sympathetic to her. I'm not, really. Just putting it down as it might have happened. There aren't any should have beens. This is the way Cathy died.

October 17, Wednesday

And Cathy died. I did well over three thousand words yesterday and built a coffee table too. Last night went to the Kazans to see Streetcar.* Really a fine film. But I was pretty sleepy. I'd like to see it again when I am a little more alert.

Since I did nearly two days' work yesterday I am just going to complete Joe today and let it go at that. Then tomorrow I'll get back to the others. I can't do too much at once. Don't want to.

We're going up to look at marble this afternoon and maybe order a piece. I have finished the mahogany coffee table and I think it is very good looking. Today is Wednesday. Tomorrow and Friday I shall lead up to my ending and next week I shall go into my ending. That will give me Saturday and Sunday to think about it. I have it all worked except of course for the exact length and some few things like that. Now I should go to work on Joe. He is really a lyric character, isn't he?—a lovable boy. But he is calling me now and I must go to him.

October 18, Thursday

If I were not so nearly finished with this volume, I would not permit myself the indiscipline of overwork. This is the falsest of economies. But since end is in view I am permitting myself the indulgence. It is two o'clock in the morning and I can't stay away from my book. Since I can't sleep anyway I might just as well be putting words down instead of only thinking them. Every other night I sleep heavily as a pig.

I'll be through pretty soon. Yesterday I wound up Kate and Joe. I am ready for the last—leading to the ending—except for one thing. I must balance the book. I feel need for proportion. This is a book unlike any other. It has a greater freedom than most and much more discipline than most. What follows in the story is a kind of envoi and before that I must prepare. In every book I have ever written, it has occurred to some readers (and I know because they have written me) to wonder where I stand in all of this. Well—this time I propose to tell them in advance. And I am ready in this. And I am going to take the means you must know in your bones is inevitable. So—now read on and see.

October 18, still Thursday, and now it is getting toward morning

And now you see, Pat, that I had to put in that last chapter to the boys. And, as you know, it is to many others besides

---

* *A Streetcar Named Desire*, from the Tennessee Williams play.

the boys. I had to say it out and honestly because that is the kind of book this is. It has no subtleties or rather, no obvious ones. Besides that, the book's form required that chapter. And I had to state my credo in plain language. Now I am ready for the last of the story. It will be straightforward and direct. It is now November and the story ends in April but there will be a jump between.

Now, having done my day's work before the day has dawned, I am going to spend the day in the garden, in painting, in making furniture. I need to work with my hands.

And there's no reason why you should not have this last part to get into type now. Maybe I'll even take it to you. But if I don't, you may come for it.

October 22, Monday

So, we go into the last week and I may say I am very much frightened. I guess it would be hard to be otherwise—all of these months and years aimed in one direction and suddenly it is over and it seems that the thunder has produced a mouse.

Last week there was complete exhaustion and very near collapse. I guess to anyone who has not worked in this way it would be hard to conceive this kind of slow accumulated weariness. I don't know any other work that requires month after month of emotional as well as intellectual concentration, although there may be some. I'm glad I took three days off. I slept a drugged sleep most of the time, and one without drugs. Wouldn't say I am much rested but I think I have the energy to finish at least.

You must be no less frightened than I because you don't know what is going to happen and all I don't know is whether I can make it happen. So in a way I am better off than you are. It is too bad we have not more humor about this. After all it is only a book and no worlds are made or destroyed by it. But it becomes important out of all proportion to its importance. And I suppose that is essential. The dunghill beetle must be convinced of the essential quality in rolling his ball of dung, and a golfer will not be any good at it unless striking a little ball is the most important thing in the world. So I must be convinced that this book is a pretty rare event and I must have little humor about it. Can't afford to have. The story has to move on and on and on.

It is like a machine now—set to do certain things. And it is about to clank to its end.

And I might just as well get to it because putting it off isn't going to help a bit.

Later. Well—there's the first day of it. And now that I am into it, it doesn't seem quite so impossible. But also I don't know how long it will be. It will have to take its own course. But I do know this. There will be no more days off until it is done.

October 23, Tuesday

The plodding goes on into the final process. And with this long a book strange things happen on the fringes. The callus on my knuckle is huge and very hard but there is a callus also large on my little finger simply from moving over the paper.

Now—yesterday's work was rather unexpected, or rather a little more developed than I had thought. There will be one change necessary. When we first see Nesbitt he will be chief deputy. He served from '03 to '19. I remember him well. He lived just around the corner from us. I'm at work early today and will probably have to work late but it doesn't matter. The scene today is a strange one—full of suggestions. It is the kind you will understand better when you come back to it. It will have things in it you won't recognize until the second time around. This is a kind of writing I like and like to do. So I think I am going to enjoy doing it. There is no harm in liking what you are doing I think. Time is moving up on me. I thought surely I would be finished this week but now I am not sure. All I know is this— I shall take no more days off until I am finished. And now is time!

October 24, Wednesday

This is going to be a hard and ferocious day and for two reasons. I have to make some tape for the Voice of America this afternoon and rewrite the material first. And that's always a hazard. Second, a very curious thing happened last night. I have been working so close to this story and last night I had a dream about the part to be written today, so complicated, so foreign and strange that I have great difficulty in shaking it off.

The dream and the reality won't seem to separate. I'm afraid I'm going to have great difficulty with that. It is very hard. Maybe I am not really enough awake yet. Too bad. The damned dream was so convincing but it just didn't belong to this book. Isn't that crazy.

Yesterday I bought a raincoat to use in Europe so I'll only have to take one coat. Also bought wood for the library doors which I will make myself. Two-inch-thick clear pine and each plank 21 inches wide. Beautiful wood. It will take me a long time to surface them and make them beautiful but I will fit and put them up very soon. Also found great brass hinges to support them. They will be a joy, and do you know, that is all the library needs. Then that room will be done. Oh! I must rebuild one part of the bookcases, but that isn't hard at all. That is a lovely room I think.

Elaine worked until midnight on manuscript and discovered that you are still sitting on the whole last part of the original. I must call you today and get that straight or she will run out of work. She is going today for shots to try to help her neck. I hope to goodness it works for the bad neck has nearly driven her crazy.

What I am trying to do is to lose that dream and I think I am about rid of it. Now I have had some more coffee and I think I am about ready to go to work. I hope I have cleared that dusty dream away. It was a bad one. I hope I don't have any more of them. So I will try.

Well there it is and I hope you will like that part. But you will tell me. And I know you can feel how the book is drawing together toward a close. One more scene here, then a kind of lyric transition and then the end.

October 25, Thursday

What a day. So beautiful and so clear and cool. But I'll sit in and do my work like a good kid. And that's not going to be finished Friday. I think perhaps Sunday—maybe Sunday but I'm not even sure of that—not even that. I've taken such care I'm not going to skimp it now. The shots of iodine have had an immediate good effect on Elaine's bad neck. I hope to goodness it works. She has not been without pain for about four years.

And that can wear you down as I well know. I have my window open and the air is like cold silk—sleek and sharp and good. It chills me a little and that I like, I like very much.

Today I need do nothing but write. Yesterday I had to write that speech and go over and record it in addition to my work. You know confusion tires me much more than work ever does. But still I think the work was good. Elaine says it was. She corrected mss. until 2 last night while I cleaned my room, really deeply cleaned it and found things that had been lost for a very long time. It was such a mess it took all evening. If my door wood comes today I may shop for brass hinges for it. There's a place on Third Avenue which might have them. But I feel pretty good and free today and even though I won't be getting finished as soon as I thought. I think I have four more days counting today. Maybe a little less—but not much. There's just too much to put down and that can't be left out. Elaine complains that Carson McCullers always gets tired and tries to resolve a book in a page.

But I'm in such a doodling mood today, so foolish. I'll never get through this way. Just playing with wood. And I can't so I might just as well give that up. Now to work

October 27 [SATURDAY]

I feel weak and miserable today as though the sky were falling on me. And maybe it is. Weariness is on me, really creeping in, and I can't give in to it. I know that sounds strange. Rest is always supposed to be good. But it would take too long and it would be too hard to get back. So—I'm going to try to go on. Sometimes I think I'm a little nuts and sometimes worse than that. I'll shake this off as soon as I can. Sounds almost as though I were sorry for myself and I really am not. Yesterday's work was no good. I had to throw it out. I made a bad mistake in saying when I would be finished and now I find myself trying to make it when I said I would. I'll have to stop that —stop it cold. The book is more important than the finish. I'll try to re-establish in my mind the fact that the book is never going to be done. That way it will move smoothly to the finish. God knows how to do this. But yesterday's work was way off.

October 29, Monday

I am not finished and I have no time limit now. I may go on all year. That time limit was the bad thing. A number of things have happened but I'm not going into that now. I'll tell you about it at some future time. Now my job is just to get as much done every day as I can and maybe in the fullness of time the book will be done.

Later. Well—there's that day. There's that day.

October 30, Tuesday

It looks now as though Nov. 1 was a good guess in the first place. Now Aron is dead and the story can draw to its close. I have two or maybe three more days to go. It seems to keep ahead. I'll probably know more tomorrow about that—tomorrow at the end of the day.

The time seems endless and yet I can't see what I can leave out of this without there being holes. But it seems endless to me. I wish I were finished and at the same time I am afraid to be finished. I wonder whether you know how that could be. Anyway that's the way it is. I'm trying to keep some kind of discipline together—as much as I can anyway. Today I have probably the hardest work in the whole book. And now I go to it.

October 31, Wednesday

The days stretch on and on. I think finally I can see the end but I am afraid to say it any more. And so I will not say. The work yesterday was good I think. The work today is going to be harsh, a good part of it. Some has to be.

Today is Halloween. I must get presents for the boys and take them up. [. . .] I am beginning to have some plan of action which I must think out very carefully.

At work early. We are putting the wallpaper in the dining room after work. I will not increase my work by one single word. So far I have kept my wordage down and I think it has a good deal to do with the pace of the book.

Now I think to work.

November 1, Thursday

Today I should be pretty close to finishing.[. . .]

You can see it is going to be a tough day. But I'll do the best I can. [. . .]

Original Draft for
the Dedication of *East of Eden*

To Pascal Covici

Dear Pat,

I have decided for this, my book, *East of Eden*, to write dedication, prologue, argument, apology, epilogue and perhaps epitaph all in one.

The dedication is to you with all the admiration and affection that have been distilled from our singularly blessed association of many years. This book is inscribed to you because you have been part of its birth and growth.

As you know, a prologue is written last but placed first to explain the book's shortcomings and to ask the reader to be kind. But a prologue is also a note of farewell from the writer to his book. For years the writer and his book have been together —friends or bitter enemies but very close as only love and fighting can accomplish.

Then suddenly the book is done. It is a kind of death. This is the requiem.

Miguel Cervantes invented the modern novel and with his Don Quijote set a mark high and bright. In his prologue, he said best what writers feel—The gladness and The terror.

"Idling reader" Cervantes wrote, "you may believe me when I tell you that I should have liked this book, which is the child of my brain, to be The fairest. The sprightliest and The cleverest that could be imagined, but I have not been able to contravene the law of nature which would have it that like begets like—"

And so it is with me, Pat. Although some times I have felt that I held fire in my hands and spread a page with shining— I have never lost the weight of clumsiness, of ignorance, of aching inability.

A book is like a man—clever and dull, brave and cowardly, beautiful and ugly. For every flowering thought there will be a page like a wet and mangy mongrel, and for every looping flight a tap on the wing and a reminder that wax cannot hold the feathers firm too near the sun.

Well—then the book is done. It has no virtue any more. The writer wants to cry out—"Bring it back! Let me rewrite it or better—Let me burn it. Don't let it out in the unfriendly cold in that condition."

As you know better than most, Pat, the book does not go from writer to reader. It goes first to the lions—editors, publishers, critics, copy readers, sales department. It is kicked and slashed and gouged. And its bloodied father stands attorney.

EDITOR

The book is out of balance. The reader expects one thing and you give him something else. You have written two books and stuck them together. The reader will not understand.

WRITER

No, sir. It goes together. I have written about one family and used stories about another family as well as counterpoint, as rest, as contrast in pace and color.

EDITOR

The reader won't understand. What you call counterpoint only slows the book.

WRITER

It has to be slowed—else how would you know when it goes fast.

EDITOR

You have stopped the book and gone into discussions of God knows what.

WRITER

Yes, I have. I don't know why. Just wanted to. Perhaps I was wrong.

EDITOR

Right in the middle you throw in a story about your mother and an airplane. The reader wants to know where it ties in and, by God, it doesn't tie in at all. That disappoints a reader.

WRITER

Yes, sir. I guess you're right. Shall I cut out the story of my mother and the airplane?

EDITOR

That's entirely up to you.

SALES DEPARTMENT

The book's too long. Costs are up. We'll have to charge five dollars for it. People won't pay five dollars. They won't buy it.

WRITER

My last book was short. You said then that people won't buy a short book.

PROOFREADER

The chronology is full of holes. The grammar has no relation to English. On page so-and-so you have a man look in the World Almanac for steamship rates. They aren't there. I checked. You've got Chinese New Year wrong. The characters aren't consistent. You describe Liza Hamilton one way and then have her act a different way.

EDITOR

You make Cathy too black. The reader won't believe her. You make Sam Hamilton too white. The reader won't believe him. No Irishman ever talked like that.

WRITER

My grandfather did.

EDITOR

Who'll believe it.

SECOND EDITOR

No children ever talked like that.

WRITER

(losing temper as a refuge from despair)

God dam it. This is my book. I'll make the children talk any way I want. My book is about good and evil. Maybe the theme got into the execution. Do you want to publish it or not?

Let's see if we can't fix it up. It won't be much work. You want it to be good, don't you? For instance the ending. The reader won't understand it.

WRITER

Do you?

EDITOR

Yes, but the reader won't.

PROOFREADER

My god, how you do dangle a participle. Turn to page so-and-so.

There you are, Pat. You came in with a box of glory and there you stand with an armful of damp garbage.

And from this meeting a new character has emerged. He is called the Reader.

THE READER

He is so stupid you can't trust him with an idea.
He is so clever he will catch you in the least error.
He will not buy short books.
He will not buy long books.
He is part moron, part genius and part ogre.
There is some doubt as to whether he can read.

Well, by God, Pat, he's just like me, no stranger at all. He'll take from my book what he can bring to it. The dull witted will get dullness and the brilliant may find things in my book I didn't know were there.

And just as he is like me, I hope my book is enough like him so that he may find in it interest and recognition and some beauty as one finds in a friend.

Cervantes ends his prologue with a lovely line. I want to use it, Pat, and then I will have done. He says to the reader:

"May God give you health—and may He be not unmindful of me, as well."

JOHN STEINBECK

New York 1952